NEVER EVER BE THE SAME

A
NEW YOU
STARTS TODAY

KATHY COLLARD MILLER | LARRY MILLER

LEAFWOOD
PUBLISHERS
an imprint of Abilene Christian University Press

NEVER EVER BE THE SAME

A New You Starts Today

LEAFWOOD
P U B L I S H E R S
an imprint of Abilene Christian University Press

Copyright © 2015 by Kathy Collard Miller and Larry Miller

ISBN 978-0-89112-450-4 | LCCN 2014042322

Printed in the United States of America

MEDICAL DISCLAIMER: The information provided is not intended to be a substitute for professional medical advice, diagnosis, or treatment. Never disregard professional medical advice, or delay in seeking it, because of something you have read in this book.

Scripture quotations, unless otherwise noted, are from The ESV® Bible (The Holy Bible, English Standard Version®) copyright © 2001 by Crossway, a publishing ministry of Good News Publishers. ESV® Text Edition: 2011. The ESV® text has been reproduced in cooperation with and by permission of Good News Publishers. Unauthorized reproduction of this publication is prohibited. All rights reserved.

Scripture quotations marked (NIV) are taken from THE HOLY BIBLE, NEW INTERNATIONAL VERSION®, NIV®. Copyright © 1973, 1978, 1984, 2011 by Biblica, Inc.® Used by permission. All rights reserved worldwide.

Scripture quotations marked NASB are taken from the NEW AMERICAN STANDARD BIBLE®, Copyright © 1960, 1962,1963, 1968, 1971, 1972, 1973, 1975, 1977, 1995 by The Lockman Foundation. Used by permission.

Scripture quotations marked (AMP) are taken from the Amplified® Bible, Copyright © 1954, 1958, 1962, 1964, 1965, 1987 by The Lockman Foundation Used by permission.

LIBRARY OF CONGRESS CATALOGING-IN-PUBLICATION DATA
Miller, Kathy C. (Kathy Collard), 1949-
  Never ever be the same : a new you starts today / Kathy Collard Miller and Larry Miller.
      pages cm
  Includes bibliographical references.
  ISBN 978-0-89112-450-4
 1. Sin--Christianity. 2. Christianity--Psychology. 3. Trust in God--Christianity. I. Title.
  BT715.M63 2015
  248.4--dc23

                                                              2014042322

Cover design by Kent Jensen | Interior text design by Sandy Armstrong, Strong Design

Leafwood Publishers is an imprint of Abilene Christian University Press
1626 Campus Court, Abilene, Texas 79601

1-877-816-4455 | www.leafwoodpublishers.com

                15 16 17 18 19 20 / 7 6 5 4 3 2 1

John and Patti Cepin
Thank you for guiding us deeper
within the arms of Jesus
where we learned to drink from
the living spring.

Acknowledgments

We are grateful to so many of our family and friends who have supported us in so many ways: reading the manuscript, talking over ideas, and praying for wisdom and guidance. Thank you to Karen Dye, Marty and Barbara Jacobus, Don and Kat Dunkle, Ron and Donna Rowell, Tim and Jeannette Wilcox, Jim and Sharon Harper, Mary Berst, Missi Jacobus, Lynnette Whitlock, Dana Rausch, and Bob and Yvonne Turnbull.

This book was influenced by the writings of Larry Crabb, Dan Allender, David Powlison, and Paul Tripp. It would never have been written nor would our lives have been changed without the books and teachings of these men. Thank you for influencing us through your writings and your examples. You laid a foundation of knowledge that we have built upon.

We are so grateful to Gary Myers, Mary Hardegree, Gene Shelburne, and the staff of Leafwood Publishing. You have caught our vision and passion and made this book possible and better with your input.

We are also grateful to those who have allowed us to walk into their lives to hear their stories and to share with them principles that we trusted the Lord would use to draw them closer to him.

God used writer and speaker Janet Thompson to open the door for us to contact Leafwood Publishers. Thank you, Janet, for following the Lord's prompting.

We are indebted to the lives and ministry of John and Patti Cepin. Your wisdom and humility to walk with us on our own journey made us thirsty to turn away from our muddy cisterns and crave the pure water of God's living spring. Thank you. We encourage our readers to check out the ministry of the Cepins at www.JourneyCompanionsMinistries.org.

Thank you, Lord, for offering and providing a safe place to draw us closer to you. And for giving us the privilege to be a part of others' lives and to write this book. Use it for your glory.

Table of Contents

Section I

The Cistern

*A*ll of us have reasons for what we do. They are *reasons*, not *excuses*. God wants to make a difference in our lives by unearthing the underlying causes. In this section, we are going to identify how and why we often respond in ungodly ways. A simple model goes a long way in explaining the unidentified causes at the root of our reactions. That model is:

> *The Wound creates a Message of Wrong Beliefs and Distorted Images, resulting in a Vow, creating a Sinful Strategy, and when the Strategy is threatened, we become Hooked.*

In this model, getting Hooked is both the beginning of the cycle and the end. It's similar to the famous query about which comes first, the chicken or the egg? When we're Hooked, we respond in an ungodly manner, which reminds us of the Wounds, which we are determined to cover up.

The elements of the model are not always apparent in every experience, and they don't always happen in this order. But this model is a helpful guide for seeing how and why we react the way we do.

After we identify the elements of this model in our lives, we will travel into Section II, The Living Spring, which provides redemption and hope in Repentance, Surrender, and the Process of Growth. If Repentance and Surrender are the desired results, you might ask, why not just skip this first section and go immediately to the next? Doing this short-circuits the possibility of true heart change. We must address the underlying foundation that gave birth to distrust of God. As we do that, each chapter builds upon the previous one.

Our passion is to help you see how you have formulated the Sinful Strategies. Seeing this will enable you to drink deeply from God's living spring.

CHAPTER 1

Why Do I Do What I Do?

*The gospel is a vital gift from God not only for our salvation
but also to enable us to deal with the ongoing activity
of sin in our lives. So we still need the gospel every day.*

—Jerry Bridges

*Only those who acknowledge that they are thirsty
ever drink from the Spring of Living Water.*

—Robert W. Kellemen

I was taking a walk with Kathy recently and she asked me,
"Larry, remember how you mentioned that you rarely prayed
when you faced a potentially dangerous situation as a police
officer? Why do you think you didn't pray?"

"Well, I would pray for the safety of other officers," I
answered, "but frankly I never gave a thought about praying for
myself. I was so confident in my training and decision-making
skills that I believed I was prepared for anything."

"That seems a little presumptuous," she replied. Then she asked
me, "Could your prayerlessness be tied to your first acting role?"

Immediately my memory flashed back to one of the most
humiliating times in my life. As a thirteen-year-old, I had a role

in the school play. I can still see myself entering from stage left. As I approached my mark and looked at the entire student body, my mind went blank. I could not speak! My heart raced. I forgot my lines. I sensed the stage prompter calling out my lines, but the only thing I heard was the swoosh of my wildly pounding heart. I stood there mute.

My meltdown completely disrupted the play, of course. The other actors came out of character. They turned and stared at me. The silence terrified me. It felt like I stood naked before all my peers. In a feeble attempt to recapture any microscopic shred of dignity, I improvised some lines and the other actors continued as I exited stage right. I have no other memories of my acting debut. I didn't want any others.

I do clearly remember my heart's conclusion: "I am worthless, weak, and vulnerable. I vow to *never* be out of control again. I will always be prepared." I never wanted to feel that pain again, and this included any emotion. Those pesky feelings that kept erupting in my heart seemed soft, weak, and way too risky because I couldn't control them. So in my personality I left no room for feelings, only for my determined efforts to excel, perform, and look good in order to feel safe. So, I tilled the soil of my heart, packed feelings down, and rolled them smooth. As the country song laments, "I stomped that sucker flat."

I turned to Kathy and said, "That is a good question about my failure to pray. I was presumptuous because I was terrified. I left no room for God in those crisis situations. My training, skill, and mastery over my job just took charge. I spent my entire life honing that Strategy of depending on myself to prevent any weakness from being exposed."

We continued chatting and the puzzle pieces began falling into place. I realized that in the inner world I had created for myself, anything that threatened my image must be handled by the only one I really trusted. Me. I had left God out of the equation so that I could maintain control. Of course, I would gladly pray for the protection of my peers. That cost me nothing. It didn't make me look weak. Maybe them, but not me.

As Kathy and I walked, I felt a sense of repentance that my prayerlessness was rooted in a rebellious spirit that instinctively rejected anything a sovereign God might place in my path. I said, "Oh, Honey, I am a wicked man. It's a good thing that I am redeemed!"

～ ～ ～

Along with some of the other ladies, I had signed up to take refreshments to our adult Sunday school class, knowing at the time that I would be out of town the week before. But I would return on Saturday, so I was available. That Saturday I listened to the messages on our voice mail. Among them were two messages from Cherie, the person in charge of refreshments. Her first message said, "Kathy, you are bringing refreshments to class this coming Sunday. Let me know that you can still do that." In the second message, Cherie said, "Kathy, I haven't heard from you, so I'm assuming you can't bring refreshments. I'll get someone else to do it."

As soon as I heard the second message, my anger went sky high. I yelled at Larry, "How dare she think I would be stupid enough to sign up for something I couldn't do. I think I'll just bring snacks anyway to show her that I keep my promises!"

Larry looked at me as if I were a mad woman. "Kathy, it's no big deal. I don't see why this bothers you so much."

"You've got to be kidding me. Of course, it bothers me. It means she thinks I don't keep my promises, that I'm a liar and stupid." I kept sputtering the same thing as if it made sense. I was too upset to examine my motives. I just knew something really dangerous was going on. But after a few days passed, I began to think more clearly about the incident. "Why, indeed, am I so bothered?" I wondered. I didn't know.

It was not until over a decade later that I discovered the underlying reason. Through examining the principles we will introduce to you in this book, I learned that my reaction of anger was a protective device to prevent me from being exposed as a liar, as undependable and stupid. Where did this come from?

When I was in third grade, I was Mrs. Leighton's "teacher's pet." Everyone knew that Mrs. Leighton favored me, and this was like drinking living water for my child's thirsty soul. Mrs. Leighton, for some reason, considered me important and worthy of her special approval.

On one particular day, I said something hurtful to someone in class, and several other students heard it. I don't remember what I said, but it was so bad that one of the students called Mrs. Leighton over and told her what had come out of my mouth. Mrs. Leighton looked at me with concern and asked, "Kathy, did you say that?"

The potential for possibly destroying what I enjoyed was being threatened. I felt like I was in a vise. The students who had heard me knew the truth. I knew the truth. All eyes were on me.

And I chose to protect what seemed like living water. I lied. "No, Mrs. Leighton, I didn't say that."

Mrs. Leighton smiled her approval—she even looked triumphant—and turned away. In that moment I concluded that I was a liar and I felt ashamed. Looking back now, I know that I made an unconscious Vow: "No one must ever know that I am a liar." I don't remember thinking those words, but the result I now see is undeniable. To mask my flaws, from that time on I became impeccably dependable.

My Strategy became dependability. "If I'm dependable, no one will know the horrible truth that I'm a liar. Dependability is the opposite of lying. If you lie, you don't keep your promises and you aren't dependable. But if you are dependable, no one can call you a liar." So, for many years, I honed the skill of dependability. My teachers described me in every report card with the affirming words, "Kathy is very dependable and conscientious." I made sure no one could ever accuse me of lying.

Over the years, I failed at times in being dependable. In those moments, anger reared its ugly head, because anger took the focus off of me and pointed the finger elsewhere. "Look at what Cherie did to me," I wanted to scream at Larry that day. "Don't look at the possibility that I'm a liar, look at her. She isn't very smart not to believe the sign-up sheet." I had the same knee-jerk reaction I had made many times over the years and then wondered later, "Why do things like that bother me so much?"

Can you relate to either of our examples? Or maybe you have your own ungodly reactions and afterward wonder, "Why do I react that way? I don't want to act in that ungodly way. I even ask God for help. I want to be holy as God desires, but I keep doing what I don't want to do."

Sucking Mud from the Cistern of Ungodliness

Jeremiah 2:13 holds a vivid picture of why we do what we do: "My people have committed two evils: they have forsaken me, the fountain of living waters, and hewed out cisterns for themselves, broken cisterns that can hold no water."

God tells Jeremiah his people are sucking mud!

When we visited Israel, we saw real cisterns. Cisterns are big holes dug out of the earth and rock. The purpose of a cistern is to store water when there isn't enough rain or a natural spring nearby. None of us can exist long without water. It is essential. You better make sure you have enough.

The problem with cisterns is that they leak, get muddy, and become polluted. Although a cistern is the best provision a human can make on his own, it is a far cry from a flowing spring of fresh water. A spring gives constant fresh water that is pure, great tasting, and never ending. A spring is preferable, but springs are rare in the desert. And a lot of the people Jeremiah is talking to are nomads. They wander around. They don't stay in one place because their flocks and herds need new grass.

So the Israelites know the difference between a cistern and a spring. They might be grateful for a cistern, even if it is muddy; but they would much rather have a fountain of fresh water.

God tells his people that spiritually, because of him, they always have a spring available for their souls. Unfortunately, the people have chosen to go to a polluted cistern and drink mud. This is not a case of a flowing spring being unavailable. God is always available for their spiritual nourishment and hydration, but they have turned away from him.

Part of the problem is that we don't experience instant death when we suck spiritual mud from a self-created cistern. We do derive some hydration for our souls. It doesn't seem that bad. Our souls are still surviving, but we don't know that our spiritual cells are begging for pure spring water. The damage does not seem all that critical, so we continue to resist God's call to holiness. Our patterns of ungodliness—anger, bitterness, discontent, lack of compassion, contempt, a critical spirit— seem like the only "drink" available. Yet at times we have drunk deeply of a living spring in fellowship with God, and at such moments we wonder, "Why can't it be like this all the time?"

Would you like to drink more often from the life-giving spring of pure water and turn away from a muddy cistern? Through a process of progressive, increasing sanctification, it can be done.

Does the challenge ever end? No, not while we are on this earth. But, through the power of the Holy Spirit, we can begin to listen more carefully to the Spirit's promptings, as he whispers, "God wants the best for you. He loves you. Surrender control of your life to him. Yes, he's calling you to selflessness. He is asking you to surrender your rights with no guarantee that you'll be taken care of. But it will be the best choice you'll ever make. With rewards in heaven to boot."

Haven't you been surrendering yourself ever since you committed your life to Christ? Of course. We want to put our hands into God's hand; we want to always go to the living spring; we want to believe God wants the best for us. And we often do. But we just keep doing the same wrong things. We're not loving. We're defensive. We want our own way. We're angry about the imperfections of others. The call of the cistern seems overwhelming.

But it really is possible to journey toward holiness by drinking more often from God's living spring. We Millers realize that we have not completed that journey, and we are not seeking or expecting to reach perfection, but we have seen the light at the end of the tunnel grow a little brighter and stronger. The cistern's muddy water seems less and less tantalizing, and the pure-flowing living stream that the Father offers is more easily chosen. Our trust in him has grown, and we are more often able to surrender to the Spirit, even when doing so feels dangerous.

Our Journey to the Spring

Our journey into greater sanctification began several years ago when we went to a seminar that offered us an opportunity to be counseled by a soul-care provider. Our eyes were opened as to how the Vows we made and the Strategies we chose and formed in our childhood had become ruts that seemed so natural and normal.

We talked about how God had used us in mighty ways, allowing us to speak nationally and internationally and to write dozens of books. Yet our counselor said things like, "That has nothing to do with Jesus." Nothing to do with Jesus? But was that not the whole reason for our efforts? Though she used hyperbole, it resonated. We knew it was true. We realized that what we thought was dependence on a flowing spring was primarily sucking mud from a cistern. While we were shocked, we also began to have more hope that the Lord could transform our motives to desire his glory.

After an extensive time of counseling, our soul-care provider said, "I'm wondering if the Lord might be calling you to a sabbatical from ministry." We fought tears as we nodded in agreement. We knew it was the Lord calling us to a time of focusing exclusively on him, free from the distractions of our writing and speaking.

She continued, "Would you want to set a goal of three months or six months?"

I spoke up first, "For me it must be open ended. And, in fact, as I go into this, I must accept the possibility of never returning to ministry."

I looked to Larry to see what he was thinking. He nodded and said, "Yes, we must be willing to release ministry altogether. It has to be the Lord calling us back, not us predetermining when it will end. Otherwise, we'll just take the time as a segment out of the normal and return to ministry as we were before."

We began the journey of greater sanctification with a sabbatical. Everything we had been doing was open for reevaluation. We were walking on a path where fog blocked our view even several steps ahead.

For the next eighteen months we spent many hours each day studying, praying, and seeking correction. The more we asked God for insight into our underlying motives, the more we faced our own selfish intentions. Those are strong words—*our own selfish intentions*—but we have continued for seven years now to have our wills broken as we have faced our impure motives. Yet, we recognize the value of what we have been experiencing. We have even begun to welcome being spiritually disciplined.

During our extended sabbatical, we were experiencing the logical, appropriate consequences that only a wise and just God could give—a God who is also completely loving and compassionate. Sometimes we saw in Scripture the ways we were trying to defend ourselves. At other times, continued counseling revealed behaviors that seemed loving but were all about making us look good. It was an intensive time of asking, "What is this about, Lord?" and thirsting for the spring of pure water.

Are we still sucking mud? Yes. A lot. But less. A lot less and with a hope and confidence that the Holy Spirit will continue in powerful ways to use the principles we have learned. Our sanctification won't stop completely while we are alive on this earth. But, as we mentioned earlier, our desire is growing for the fountain of living, pure water rather than the mud of a broken cistern.

Are You Sucking Mud?

Our passion and goal is that you will learn how to thirst for God and forsake the broken cistern. And then that you will learn new, holy responses based in drinking deeply of God's living spring.

Will you journey with us? We are whispering in your ear, "Go to God! He offers life. It will be hard, but the journey of sanctification is worth it. The journey may be challenging, but its destination is victory and freedom."

Ask Yourself These Questions

To begin our journey together, we would like for you to answer several questions. Please write your answers in the space provided. There are no wrong or right answers. You can write as much or as little as you want. Don't try to figure out the "best" answers, but do answer from your heart. Usually whatever comes to mind first is from your heart.

As we have posed these same questions to those who come to us for soul care, their answers greatly reveal the underlying motives in their hearts. If you are serious about wanting to have a true heart change, we have confidence it can happen. These simple questions are a first step.

1. What does it seem like or feel like you should have?

2. What do you hate?

3. What have you promised yourself?

4. How do you hate being seen by others?

5. What would you like to avoid at all costs?

6. Who has hurt you the most?

7. What instruction in the Bible do you have trouble obeying or understanding?

8. If something could be changed in your life to make you happy, what would it be?

9. What three things, people, or circumstances bring you the most happiness?

10. If you could change one person's opinion or perception of you, who would it be and what would it be?

11. When you are not happy, what do you do for escape?

12. Who are you determined not to be like?

13. Aside from Jesus, who do you want to be like?

Your answers are important in helping you put the principles of this book into practice. We will refer back to your answers in many of the chapters to help make these concepts intensely personal and applicable.

Are you longing to know Christ more fully? Are you longing to have a heart less divided by ungodly motives? Are you longing to take hold of God's power for responding in godly ways?

Come with us on this journey called holiness. It is not easy, and it is a continual process, but it is our calling from God; therefore, it must be possible.

Reflections and Group Discussion Questions

1. To what degree do you feel hopeful about making changes in your life?

2. When you think of holiness, what do you think and feel?

3. How do you define sanctification?

4. What are the desires of your heart for greater holiness?

5. Have you ever wondered, "Why do I do what I do?" Describe the feelings that go along with that thought.

6. Look at the opening paragraphs of this chapter. If there were an opening paragraph written about you and your current situation, what would it say?

7. Were you familiar with Jeremiah 2:13 before you read it here? How does it speak to you?

8. Do you have ideas of what motivates you when you:

   • disobey God?
   • obey God?

9. Which of your answers to these questions at the end of this chapter:

    •   surprise you?
    •   delight you?
    •   perplex you?
    •   make you curious?

10. If you feel comfortable, read to the group some of your answers to these questions. Which of the questions is hardest to answer? Why do you think so?

11. How would you like to be empowered by the Holy Spirit in a new way?

Chapter 2

The Hook

*The thing we place our hope in will influence
the way we interpret and respond to life.*

—Paul David Tripp

*When someone else's actions or statements threaten to pull
me into a bad place, I have a choice. I do. It may not feel like
it. In fact, it may feel like I am a slave to my feelings—but
I'm not. Remember, feelings are indicators, not dictators.*

—Lysa TerKeurst

Several years ago, my primary challenge was caring for
my mom, Audrey, in our home. She had Lewy body dementia
(LBDA.org) which includes paranoia, delusions, and hallucinations. Not only did she ask God, "Why on earth do you keep me
here?" but Kathy and I wondered about that ourselves. Now we
know. Although she passed away when she was ninety-three,
we still remember vividly how God used her in our lives to
change us.

When my mom was still living alone, the hallucinations
started disrupting her life. One day I received her frantic call
urging us to hurry over to her home. When Kathy and I drove

up, we found my mom waiting in the garage with a furious look on her face. She began yelling, "They are holding the trash cans shut. I can't open them." I walked over and opened the lids to both cans. She had tried to open them from the attached side.

She became even more enraged. "They are tormenting me!" she screamed. "They must have left before you drove up." I calmly explained that she was hallucinating again. As she raised her voice, I raised mine. (Looking back on this exchange, I wonder which one of us was really the most demented.) Kathy just stood there shocked. I was now officially "Hooked" (we'll explain shortly) by my mother's raging determination to assert her will over mine. Everything within me demanded, "Why can't she just listen to my wise counsel?" I took charge and increased my efforts to dominate my mother's illness.

As I reflect on the argument between the temporarily demented person (me!) and a permanently demented one, I realize now that I felt exposed as weak. When my mother resisted my help, I felt powerless, and I slipped into my default mode of trying to control. Anger made me feel powerful and seemed to put the blame on my mother.

My sense of weakness also included longing for my mother to approve and acknowledge the care I was giving her. My competence, assertiveness, and conflict resolution skills worked for me on the streets as a policeman, but they were strategies that now failed me in this important personal relationship. The pain I felt and the weakness the pain exposed shockingly broadsided me with the unnerving awareness that I would never look good to my mother again. My efforts to change my mother were really a demand to be recognized as coming through for her. Although I didn't realize it in the heat of that garbage-can confrontation, her approval and appreciation were more important and influential to me than God's approval. How she saw me mattered more to me than how God viewed my service.

Caught Ya! You're Hooked!

My experience with my mom is what we call being "Hooked." Unfortunately, we all experience it. Being Hooked is when we react to any aggravation or pressure in life in an ungodly way, and any ungodly reaction is sin. It's when we don't depend upon the Holy Spirit and, as a result, we react in a way that is not aligned with the fruit of the Spirit (Gal. 5:22–23).

For instance:

- Instead of being loving, we are apathetic, maybe even hateful. We rescue, people-please, and basically don't want the best for the other person. We might even punish through withdrawal.
- Instead of being joyful, we are unhappy, discontented, disgruntled, and ungrateful.
- Instead of being peaceful, we are unsettled, worried, and tense.
- Instead of being patient, we are frustrated and have unrealistic expectations.
- Instead of being kind, we are mean-spirited and critical, unsympathetic and lacking in compassion. Our actions are rough and disrespectful of another person's dignity.
- Instead of being good, we are selfish and self-centered, demanding our own way.
- Instead of being gentle, we are harsh and disregard the emotions and needs of others.

- Instead of being faithful, we are dishonest, disloyal, and undependable.
- Instead of having self-control, we are reckless, out of control, and held in bondage by anything that seems to make our life better.

We react in these ways because we don't trust God enough to surrender to whatever he desires. We take matters into our own hands. We regard as the problem whatever and whoever seems to be making our life difficult or uncomfortable. We look at that problem and think, "If only I could solve this problem, things would be good. Then I could put life back on cruise control."

The Problem Is Not the Problem

But the "presenting" problem is not the real problem. By "presenting," we mean that which we identify as the problem and which we set out to resolve because we think that doing so will get us what we want—whether it is love, happiness, joy, or peace, or maybe just someone understanding us. But when we only try to solve the presenting problem, we are focusing on behavior. God is not so much interested in our behavior as in our hearts' motives. Instead of looking just at *what* we do, he focuses on *why* we do it. A pure heart produces behavior that pleases him.

Of course, God wants us to obey him, but out of a heart that is motivated by the right reason—his glory—and not just to get the comfort and relief we crave. God desires us to have hearts like David's when he requested, "Search me, O God, and know my heart! Try me and know my thoughts! And see if there be any grievous way in me, and lead me in the way everlasting!" (Ps. 139:23–24).

The heart is where the underlying causes of our ungodly reactions arise. God longs to draw us closer to him, and he uses the pain, discomfort, or struggles we experience to motivate us to purify our hearts. Then when we draw closer to him, our behavior changes (Ezek. 36:26–27).

For many years as the two of us dealt with the problems of those we ministered to, we heard them say things like, "My husband doesn't tell me he loves me. I need his love in order to be happy. How can I get him to tell me he loves me?"

Or, "I'm always getting angry at my kids (or coworker or elderly parent or whoever is upsetting them). Tell me how I can control my anger."

All we knew to do was to advise, "six ways to conquer your anger" or "five ways to get your spouse to love you." And God used that advice in his gracious love. But we always felt like something was not being unearthed. We were digging three inches into their hearts by giving a few tips or guidelines, while sin lay hidden deep within. Then we wondered why they returned to the sinful behavior after a temporary change. We were struggling to help them with the "presenting" problem but not with the underlying source. We didn't realize we were encouraging them to suck mud from that ol' cistern while the living spring flowed nearby.

For instance, if a husband complains that his wife doesn't keep the house clean, our natural reaction is to tell him to communicate more clearly and with greater love his need for a clean house. Although it can be of some value, such advice does not touch what God might want to do in that man's life.

Most of the time the purpose of giving advice like "three ways to motivate your wife" is to help this husband to influence, even control, his wife to meet his needs so that he can be happy.

His motive is to relieve his own pain or discomfort, not to grow closer to God through trusting him more.

Instead, we needed to ask that husband, "Why has God allowed this struggle in your life?" God's plan might be for him to learn something from his wife's lack of attention that he cannot learn any other way.

A Different Perspective

"The problem isn't the problem" is exactly what God was inviting me to learn as I helped care for Larry's mother.

Every morning I fixed Audrey's breakfast of toast, coffee, and bran-flake cereal in milk. On one morning, after she pushed away her half-eaten bowl, Audrey said, "Kathy, you put too much cereal and not enough milk in the bowl. I couldn't finish it because it got too dry."

Now as soon as I hear her say "you," my anger starts to burn. I'm being blamed. She is unhappy and I can't do anything right. I can *never* please her. She's just a mean old woman who won't appreciate my wonderful care. I think everyone should know how abused I am.

Then I began to regard the situation through the filter of "the problem isn't the problem." I could see that God wanted to sanctify me, and when I got Hooked, he was pointing out my lack of trust in him. The solution was not gritting my teeth and smiling. And it was not explaining to Audrey that I did the best I could and she should be grateful.

Instead, I needed to realize, "I'm being Hooked. I want to lash out and defend myself or put the blame on her for being ungrateful." But if it is true that the problem is not the problem, I can ask the Lord, "What are you inviting me into, Lord? What is really going on in my heart?"

The key to my improper response is in my thinking that I can never please her. I am trying to gain her approval when I should be looking to God for his approval and his pleasure in my service. I am actually drinking from the muddy cistern of People-Pleasing when God wants me to come to him to drink of his life-giving freshwater flow. He wants to stamp "Well done, good and faithful servant" on me, but I push it aside and say, "I want it from Audrey." In fact, the truth is that this has been my desire since I became her daughter-in-law.

For me, God's call of holiness in the most recent years has been teaching me to seek what only God can provide: a true reflection of my worth and value based upon Jesus' death on the cross for me. It is only found fully in the gospel of grace where unconditional love and acceptance are found through God's offer of forgiveness.

That requires being honest when we are being Hooked and everything inside us denies it. All of us are experts at denial. Here are some examples of the ways we can deceive ourselves and justify our bad habits:

- That really doesn't bother me. I raise my voice because I'm Italian.
- My mother doesn't hook me. I've just grown weary of her nagging.
- Of course, my son's drug problem worries me. Any parent would be worried.
- I'm not trying to get her approval; I just think I should be respected like the Bible commands a wife.
- I'm not trying to control my daughter; I just know what's good for her.

It is hard to acknowledge that we are Hooked and not glorifying God. Jeremiah 17:9 tells us, "The heart is deceitful above all things, and desperately sick; who can understand it?" Our resistance to acknowledging our ungodly reactions certainly reveals this. Someone can even have several people point out a sinful reaction and the guilty person will offer an excuse. All of us have been there, and often it takes time to become honest. But truth telling is freeing. From it God can transform even the most resistant heart. This is God's call to us all: "You will seek me and find me, when you seek me with all your heart" (Jer. 29:13).

Where Is Hooking in Scripture?

Let's find examples of Hooking in Scripture.

The brother/sister team Aaron and Miriam were Hooked when they criticized Moses. They *claimed* they were upset about "the Cushite woman whom he had married" (Num. 12:1), but it is pretty obvious that their deeper motive was jealousy. They complained, "'Has the LORD indeed spoken only through Moses? Has he not spoken through us also?' And the LORD heard it" (12:2). The word "only" reveals their jealousy. They demanded acknowledgment of their ministry involvement and became Hooked into criticizing Moses.

Another obvious example is Haman in the book of Esther. Haman hated Mordecai the Jew. Esther 3:5 tells us, "When Haman saw that Mordecai did not bow down or pay homage to him, Haman was filled with fury." Haman was Hooked because of his pride. He may have felt belittled, embarrassed, and insignificant. He must have felt as though the whole world was watching Mordecai's disrespect. The truth he feared was indeed being revealed. He really was not all that important or brilliant after all. So he reacted in rage that eventually fueled his plan to kill Mordecai and all the Jews.

Now let's find an example where someone resists getting Hooked. How about Daniel's three friends? King Nebuchadnezzar is requiring everyone to bow to his golden image, but not everyone is cooperating. When the king finds out that Shadrach, Meshach, and Abednego refuse to bow down, the king reacts in rage. Oh, *he* gets Hooked! Like Haman, he isn't getting the respect he craves and demands. When he calls the three young men before him, they know the consequences of not obeying the king's edict. Their lives are on the line. These three men should be terrified. They should be Hooked into anxiety bordering on terror.

Worry or anxiety on any level happen when we are Hooked because we are not trusting God. Worry is different than fear. Fear may be a legitimate reaction in a dangerous situation. (After all, if a bear meets you in the forest, you will be afraid and need to take action.) But worry is when fear turns into distrust of God. Those three young men in Babylon could be consumed with worry for their lives. But if they are, they don't show it. How do they prevent being Hooked?

> Shadrach, Meshach, and Abednego answered and said
> to the king, "O Nebuchadnezzar, we have no need
> to answer you in this matter. If this be so, our God
> whom we serve is able to deliver us from the burning
> fiery furnace, and he will deliver us out of your hand,
> O king. But if not, be it known to you, O king, that we
> will not serve your gods or worship the golden image
> that you have set up." (Dan. 3:16–18)

Their trust in God's sovereignty and their total surrender to God's will empowers them to resist being Hooked. They stay calm and peaceful; the fruit of the Spirit reigns in their lives.

Miriam, Aaron, Haman, and the king reacted in ungodly ways, but Daniel's friends did not. What is significant is that for each of these characters there was something that motivated their reactions. Miriam and Aaron were jealous. Haman was embarrassed. The king felt threatened. But Daniel's friends didn't succumb to any of those Wrong Beliefs. Instead they trusted God.

That's the challenge for each of us. To identify our motives and evaluate whether we are trusting God. The first step when we somehow lose our cool is not excusing our reactions with the rationale that getting Hooked is natural but not supernatural.

Getting Hooked Is Natural but Not Supernatural

We resist acknowledging we are Hooked (or that we are headed that way) because our reaction seems so natural. It feels like we have no other option. After all, isn't it natural and expected for us to become upset and hurt when someone offends us? Is it not natural and expected for us to become defensive when someone criticizes us? Isn't it natural and expected for us to worry when our child is late getting home? In all honesty, our bad habit (whichever one it is) just does not seem that bad. We defend ourselves by asking, "How can God call some behavior sin when we can't resist doing it? I don't have a choice."

It may be true that these bad habits are "natural," but it is just as true that God has called us to *supernatural* living. The "natural reaction" comes from our "old self" (Eph. 4:22), but we have become new creations in Christ (2 Cor. 5:17). We do not have to react in the old sinful ways because the Holy Spirit is available to empower us for a godly way.

That is the conclusion Heather came to, but not without some struggle. I had the opportunity to talk with her during the Saturday afternoon free time where I was speaking at a women's retreat.

After we settled ourselves in the chairs of my room, Heather declared, "I'm so frustrated with my mother. I have hardly spoken to her this last year. I've done so much for her, and it never does any good. I've helped her organize her house numerous times. I've helped her get out of financial messes. If she would just follow my directions, I wouldn't be so frustrated. And don't get me going about my sisters who never help me. They make me mad too!"

I asked her, "How far back does this go?"

"Even as young as five I was supposed to take care of my younger brother and sister while my parents did who knows what. Both my parents worked; I was supposed to make sure nothing bad happened at home."

I prayed silently, asking the Lord to give me insights. "How did that make you feel?"

"I didn't have any choice, so I just accepted it. Because if I didn't step up to the plate, who knows what screwy things might happen, especially to my mom."

"Heather, even though I asked you how you felt, you didn't refer to feelings. You talked about not having a choice."

"Well, yeah! What else could I do? I was a little kid."

"Yes, that's true. But would you say that's still going on? Do your feelings indicate you still think you have no choice but to help your mom and then feel angry about it?"

Heather looked confused. "My mom was always saying, 'If you don't help me, I'll kill myself.' I grew up thinking I was responsible for my mom's sanity. Of course, I didn't understand that then, but I do now."

37

I prayed for God's wisdom to put the puzzle pieces together. "Heather, does it still feel like you're responsible for your mom's sanity?"

Heather's eyes suddenly filled with tears and she dropped her head. "I guess so. What would happen if she died and I hadn't helped her?"

"Heather, who is responsible for your mom's decisions?"

"I am!" Heather blurted out, and then paused. "Well, at least that's what it feels like."

I smiled. "I understand. But you're getting Hooked because you're believing a lie that you are responsible. Have you ever considered that she is responsible for her decisions, and you are responsible for yours?"

"But it doesn't feel like it. If only she would do what I say, I wouldn't be feeling so angry."

"I know that's what you've always believed, but it's not true. You can't really say that your mom makes you feel frustrated. You are responsible for your own responses. Think of Moses. Moses was responsible for his decision to hit the rock to bring forth water for the Israelites. But God told him to speak to it."

I started turning the pages of my Bible to Numbers 20. "Moses had to shepherd the most aggravating group of people in history through the wilderness. Thousands of people resisted his leadership, grieved God with their lack of faith, and attacked Moses personally as a man and leader."

"Yeah. And wasn't that about the time that Moses had just buried his sister and the Israelites were really complaining about being thirsty?"

"That's right. Would you have felt justified getting angry at all those rebellious people and hitting the rock, especially in the midst of grieving for your sister?"

"Well, sure. A person can only stand so much."

"I can understand that because I've often justified the way I act, too. But, Heather, here's what God said about what Moses had done."

I found Numbers 20:12–13 and read, "'But the LORD said to Moses and Aaron, 'Because you have not believed Me, to treat Me as holy in the sight of the sons of Israel, therefore you shall not bring this assembly into the land which I have given them''" (NASB).

"Just think, Heather," I continued, "if anyone had a right to take personally the rejection of thousands of people, it was Moses. If anyone had a right to defend himself, it was him. And in the midst of his grief, it would seem that was more than anyone could, or should, take. It would be easy to justify his frustration. But did God justify it and tell him, 'It's okay. I understand, Moses. It's been a bad day'?"

Heather gave a little laugh. "No, he held him responsible for his actions."

"How does that speak to you?"

Heather looked a little sheepish. "Well, I guess I'm responsible for my reactions to my mom and sisters. I guess it's true that I'm choosing the way I respond."

When I asked her if she would like to pray, Heather agreed. As she sat for a moment in silence, I suggested that she ask the Lord for a mental picture of what was going on. Maybe two minutes passed before she gave a little gasp. "Oh, Lord, you're showing me a picture of my mom and sisters holding strings attached to me as if I'm a puppet. And now you're cutting the strings. They don't have to control me. Or rather, I don't have to allow them to control me. You want to empower me to live in joy and love. I can make godly choices through your Holy Spirit.

Please forgive me for making my mom and sisters more important than your opinion of me. I've sinned against you. I haven't believed you, just like Moses didn't. I receive your forgiveness and cleansing. Oh, thank you!"

When she finished praying, the tears in her eyes could not drown the smile on Heather's face. I knew she had begun an important first step in her breakthrough to a changed life.

Do you sometimes feel like Heather? Maybe you believe that you need your circumstances or someone to change in order for you to have godly reactions—and in order to not be Hooked.

Recognizing that we are responsible for our own responses is a crucial first step in having a true heart change that will transform our lives, empower us for greater holiness, and break down the barriers blocking intimacy with God. And we will be able to resist being Hooked.

Do you hunger to drink more often from God's flowing spring and experience the fruit of the Spirit? Fresh water is waiting for you.

. . . .

Reflections and Group Discussion Questions

1. Look at the list of the fruit of the Spirit in Galatians 5 and
    the accompanying ways of being Hooked (pages 29–30).
    Which of those are common in your life? Which one
    would you most like to change?

2. In consideration of what you have read in this chapter,
    look back at your answers to the questions at the end of
    Chapter One. Do you see any insights into the ways you
    are being Hooked? For instance, if what you feel like you
    must have (Question 1) seems to be withheld, how do you
    react?

3. Memorize Jeremiah 2:13. Can you identify how you have
    been drinking from muddy cisterns instead of thirsting
    for God's living spring of water?

4. Query two or three friends or relatives about any ungodly
    reactions they have noticed in you that you might be
    blind to.

5. How would James 1:2–5 suggest that God is using some-
    thing or someone painful in your life to draw you closer
    to him?

6. What reasons have you heard from others when they
    wanted to justify their bad behavior?

7. What is God currently using in your life to transform you? What has been your response to his efforts?

8. When you examine your current struggle in light of "the problem isn't the problem," what does God seem to be doing?

Chapter 3

The Wound

*Denial fuels the myth that time heals
all wounds. But memory knows no time.*

—Lindsey and Justin Holcomb

*The work of restoration cannot
begin until a problem is fully faced.*

—Dan Allender

Four years after my acting debacle, I vividly remember solidifying my resolve to protect myself and control my life. During my senior year of high school in Downey, California, I joined the water polo team. One day we were practicing and, as usual, the head coach was yelling at us. Soon his scorn was pointed at me. "You are guarding him like a sissy, Larry. Control your opponent! Get tough!" he screamed.

When my teammate made a move I couldn't counter, the coach blew his whistle, threw down his clipboard, pulled off his shirt, and jumped into the water next to me. His face flushed with anger as he scolded me, "You're too soft. Do it like this."

He reached over, stuck his finger in the side of my swimsuit, and twisted for control. "You grab him like this!" I was

43

surprised when he dunked me and thereby demonstrated to the entire team how to skillfully cheat.

When I was jerked down, I had not had time to grab a breath. As he held me under, I was desperate to breathe. After he pulled me up, instantly he jerked me below the water again before I could inhale any air. Panic surged through me. I struggled wildly, trying to claw my way to the surface, but he was too strong. I felt powerless to protect myself.

Again he brought me back up briefly and I managed a partial breath before he jerked me down a third time. Panic deteriorated into terror as he brought me up and down two more times. Moments before I passed out, convinced I would drown, he released his death grip. I shot to the surface gasping wildly for breath. I watched him pull himself out of the pool as he smirked, "Now, that is the way you dominate your opponent." None of my teammates said a thing. Nothing. Silence filled the pool area. Some friends stared at me, while others turned away.

Shame—deep, piercing shame like an icy hand—clutched my heart. It crushed my soul. I wanted to disappear, but there was nowhere to hide.

That coach stole something from me that afternoon. He took away my only strategy to make sense of life. He exposed my Vow to be in control. The message I heard from him was, "Larry, you are weak—not really a man. You don't have what it takes; you are drowning in life." It felt like I was stripped naked before my peers for all the world to see that I was weak, powerless, and unprepared.

My anger kindled by his abuse burned for many years. I never spoke of it for thirty-eight years because I was so ashamed. But something happened in that pool that was more damaging than the shame. I left that pool determined to exercise my will to protect myself at all costs. I would be a man. I would be strong. Strength and control would be my fig leaves for the rest of my life.

What I experienced fits the model we're using in this book. Here's a summary:

- *The Wound:* Feeling terrorized due to almost being drowned.
- *The Message*: You are not a man. You are weak.
- *The Belief and Image*: God cannot be trusted. I do not have what it takes.
- *The Vow*: I will be in control in order to prove that I am a man.
- *Self-Protective Sinful Strategy*: Police work makes it possible for me to be in control.
- *Hooking:* I refuse offers of friendship because I cannot allow others to know the real, weak me.

It never had occurred to me how those early experiences of pain steered me toward my career in law enforcement. When police officers are trained—from the first day—an overarching doctrine is drilled into their heads. "You must be in control at all times. You will be responsible and prepared because when you are not, people die. You must come through for yourself and others."

Wow, this was a career made just for me. Someone paid me to do the thing I thought most important: be in control. It seemed like letting a kid loose in a candy store. I could live out my Vow of self-protection. By the time I hit the streets as a rookie officer, trusting myself was a fine-tuned art. It never occurred to me to seek God, because I was too busy living life on my terms. It seemed to work.

Unfortunately, I didn't use my strategy of being in control just on the job. I tried to protect myself at all times. I distanced myself from other people with a superior attitude, because interacting with them might threaten my ability to stay in control and then I would be exposed as weak. I covered over that selfish strategy by deceiving myself that other people offered me nothing I couldn't provide for myself.

That's how I got Hooked. Now let Kathy tell you how it happened to her.

I grew up in a kid-friendly neighborhood where we played baseball in the street and had lots of friends. One of our common activities was giving consequences when one of us lost a game like hide-and-seek. One day I lost the game and it was my turn to crawl on the ground through everyone's legs while they spanked me.

Feeling embarrassed but laughing along with everyone else, I scrambled as quickly as possible on my hands and knees through the spread legs of ten children. All of the spanks were gentle pats. But almost at the end of the line, I felt someone's finger press purposefully and forcefully against my clothing into the opening of my rectum.

Horror shot through me. When I reached the end of the line, I jumped up and yelled, "I have to go home now." Shame coursed over me like a heavy wet blanket, weighing me down as I ran. Brushing tears off my cheeks, I berated myself, "Kathy, you should have prevented that from happening. See what happens when you're not careful?"

When I reached home, I rushed past my mother and ran into my bedroom, slamming the door behind me. Trying to wrap myself into an invisible ball, I told myself over and over again, "Why didn't you see it coming? Be more careful! Be more careful! I don't ever want to feel that way again."

I didn't realize it at the time, but I also had traveled through our "model."

- *The Wound:* Being molested.
- *The Message*: You are responsible. It is your fault.
- *The Belief and Image*: I did not prevent that; therefore I am dirty and shameful.
- *The Vow*: I will be hypervigilant and make sure nothing like this ever happens again.
- *Self-Protective Sinful Strategy*: Perfectionism. Since I'm dirty and shameful, I'll act perfectly and no one will know the truth about me.
- *Hooking*: When someone says something that indicates I am less than perfect, I become angry.

As a result, situations like the time when Cherie assumed I wouldn't bring snacks made me angry. In my mind I was being exposed as imperfect.

What Is a Wound?

What we have given here are examples of Wounds and the way they contribute to our Strategy formations. Larry's swim coach and Kathy's nameless neighbor child inflicted Wounds. In our first chapter, Kathy told how she inflicted a Wound on herself by lying, and Larry, in a sense, Wounded himself by forgetting his lines. All of these are examples of some level of pain. And, for us as children, life is filled with pain as well as all its joys. We might initially believe that only really painful Wounds significantly affect us, but a Wound is a Wound. They come in a variety of degrees and thus affect us to varying degrees.

The Bible shows us examples of childhood Wounds.

Isaac and Rebekah each favored one of their twins. From early childhood, Esau and Jacob felt the sting of being favored by one parent and disregarded as unimportant by the other.

Samson's parents were indulgent. They gave in to his whims and desires, neglecting to teach him self-control.

Samuel was given away by his mother, Hannah. Samuel saw his mother once a year. Did he wonder why she gave him up? Even if he were told the reason, a child could still feel the sting. Yet, he didn't allow his Wound to prevent him from loving and serving God with honor.

Joseph was favored by his father, and his brothers hated him. Joseph is a wonderful example of trusting in God regardless of unfair circumstances and the deep Wounds of being sold into slavery and being falsely accused.

All these men and women of the Bible were responsible for the choices they made. Being Wounded does not take away our responsibility for our choices. But often people are not aware of the impact their Wounds had on them.

So many times, when we hear the deep Wounds of those we talk with, we react with shock. Yet, the man we are talking to may seem unfazed by the horror of his experience. "What's wrong?" he may want to know. "Why are you so sad and distressed? It wasn't that bad. It was just the way life was."

Or a woman may describe to us the sexual abuse she suffered as a little girl. While we respond with righteous anger toward her perpetrator, she replies, "Oh, it wasn't that bad. I know of others who were abused even more severely. It doesn't bother me anymore."

Whether our Wounds are horrendous or minimal, they affect us in some way. I can only remember my dad getting angry at me one time, but it affected me deeply. "Larry," he had repeatedly told me, "put away that fire engine"; but I kept playing with it. Finally, he grabbed the metal toy, stomped into my room, and threw the fire engine across the room. It broke into unfixable pieces, and I concluded in that instant that my dad was not a safe person. From then on I approached him with less trust, regardless of his delight in me. It was only one incident—and one which does not seem that bad in hindsight—yet it communicated something significant to my little boy's heart.

Every child experiences hurtful things. No child exists who is not affected by the people who love him poorly. As we will learn, each Wound affects us in different ways. As children, we don't know how to deal with the incorrect Messages, Beliefs, and Vows that assail us. Our coping skills are limited, and we believe our conclusions are accurate. And most importantly, we Vow, "I will prevent pain like that in the future! I never want to feel that way again."

All of this gets even more complicated, because the same experience can affect people in different ways. A brother and sister may have suffered the same trauma, and each of them may respond differently. Each will form a unique set of responses depending upon personality and previous life experiences. But regardless, the desire is always the same: to avoid pain at all costs.

Avoid Pain at All Costs

We each learn creative ways to avoid pain. For examples of this, just watch reality television programming. One evening we watched the program *Hoarding: Buried Alive*. One episode featured a woman whose house was literally filled with food. In the interview, she mentioned that as a child she did not have a variety of food to eat. She explained, "Now I make sure I always have a variety of food available." Unfortunately, she also never threw away any morsel of food. She was committed to avoiding the pain of not having a variety of food—regardless of how inedible.

Another show is *What Not To Wear*. Hosts Stacy and Clinton help "regular" people receive a fashion makeover. Women on the show frequently will mention some kind of emotional pain from childhood. Although no obvious effort is made to bring emotional healing, the woman often is able to change her wardrobe "vision" as Stacy and Clinton help her find clothes that suit her. In one episode, a woman admits to hiding behind baggy clothes with bland colors. She says, "I guess I don't want to be seen." At one point, a huge birthmark on the back of one of her legs can be seen. Although the birthmark is not addressed on the show, we wondered if it could be that the teasing she received about it as a child contributed to her not wanting to be seen.

A third example is the television program *Clean Sweep*. In this program, organizers help a person or a family to clean up their cluttered home. In one episode we meet a woman who, amidst a vast collection of other clutter, hoards thousands of photos, far more than most of us could ever accumulate in three lifetimes. When she is asked why she has such an inordinate number of photos, she replies, "I was abandoned as a child, and I swore that I would make sure my children had memories. I never had photos of my childhood so I committed to having photos of our family activities for my children." She begins to cry. Fortunately, during the process of working with the hosts, she relinquishes her desperate need for such an enormous collection of pictures and is able to throw some away.

Although we may not always be able to connect our current struggles with childhood Wounds, when the Holy Spirit reveals the links, deep healing can happen.

Identifying but Not Blaming

Reviewing our Wounds does not mean that we are blaming those who hurt us. This might sound amazing, even shocking. After all, why would we rehearse the Wounds if not to say, "I am acting the way I am now because of what that person did to me? It's their fault."

That was certainly Ken's response when I met with him for soul care. When I explained that one of my goals was to help identify his childhood Wounds, Ken grinned in agreement.

"What's that grin about, Ken?" I inquired.

"I just knew my struggles were not my fault, Larry. My parents were abusive, and that's why I have the Strategies you're talking about. If only they had treated me better, I wouldn't be tempted like I am today."

Ken's wide-eyed look of expectation almost made me feel sorry for him. I knew he would be disappointed at my response.

"No, Ken, actually that's not true," I explained. "Although your parents could have treated you better, you are responsible totally for your reactions today."

Ken's grin dissipated into a disappointed grimace.

I continued, "You were mistreated, as every child is to some degree, but each of us chooses to avoid pain by depending on a particular way to cope. God offers us his godly methods, but we tend to choose our own willful ones that leave him out."

Ken's face lit up again. "I wasn't even a Christian when I chose ungodly ways to react as a child. I'm not responsible for that, right? I can see that if I'd been a Christian, then I would be responsible for wrong patterns, but I wasn't."

I smiled to myself. I had even tried to use this reasoning myself.

"I'm sorry to burst your bubble, Ken, but God was there available to you. Sure, as a child you were not expected to be perfect, but the bottom line is, regardless of what you chose as a child, you are choosing to depend upon your Self-Protective Strategies—right now as an adult. That's what God wants to change because he's available to you now."

"And what if I can't connect my current Strategies to my childhood Wounds?"

"You may not always be able to make a connection, but if the Lord wants you to do so, he'll give the insights. Regardless, the Lord holds you responsible for choosing godliness now in his power."

I went on to explain to Ken that we are not rehearsing the Wound in order to cast blame upon others, thus excusing ourselves. We are seeing how the Wound affected us and then how we chose a Self-Protective response that fosters distrust of God. But, ultimately, God wants us to forgive those who hurt us, as much for our good as for theirs, for this empowers us to turn from those Strategies.

Even Good Events Create Self-Protective Sinful Strategies

I remember the day when as an eight-year-old girl I overheard my aunt say at a family gathering, "Look how nicely Kathy is sitting. She's such a good little girl." Those affirming words were like springs of living water that my thirsty soul lapped up. Of course, I was sucking mud, but I didn't know that. Her words fed my need for approval, which my parents gave me—but never enough to fill me up.

The Message from her comment was, "Be good and you'll get approval." Therefore I Vowed, "I must look for ways to be good."

Years later I belonged to an organization for teenage girls. Once a year we spent a weekend in a mountain cabin. At the end of the weekend, one of the adult chaperones announced, "We've never done this before, but we want to give a special thank you to Diane who so selflessly helped in the kitchen." Everyone clapped as Diane went forward to receive her gift.

My immediate thought was, "If I'd known there was a gift for it, I would have helped in the kitchen too. Next time, I'll do that."

My sinful motives replaced any need to look to God to provide approval. My Vow to be hypervigilant to avoid pain and seek approval had found another method to lap at the cistern of muddy water.

Even though I went to church, my misguided "success" at finding human sources of approval contributed to believing I needed to be good enough to earn God's love. I applied my hypervigilance to my spirituality and tried to do everything perfectly, since in my mind the Lord held an ax over my head waiting for me to do something wrong. Yet I didn't feel his love. He was not "dancing" to my hypervigilant "tune," and I didn't know the right melody to play to get his applause.

In some ways I was like the Israelites God spoke to in Malachi 3:13–15.

Your words have been hard against me, says the LORD. But you say, "How have we spoken against you?" You have said, "It is vain to serve God. What is the profit of our keeping his charge or of walking as in mourning before the Lord of hosts? And now we call the arrogant blessed. Evildoers not only prosper but they put God to the test and they escape."

Larry Crabb, in *Finding God,* explains these verses:

> The Jews were saying something like this: "There really is no point in doing things God's way. Nothing we do seems to make him feel obligated to make life go as we want. So, even though we may be angry and uncertain of how to get along with ourselves and others, we're still better off trusting our own resources as we try to make it in this crazy world. Blessed are the arrogant; happy people are ones who depend on themselves."

I also wanted to manipulate God to acknowledge my efforts to be good, thus negating his grace. I was angry that my efforts were not appreciated and didn't give me the approval I needed.

Kathy was not the only one in our house who learned to increase her efforts to manage life her own way because of a good experience.

I remember my first police pursuit as if it happened yesterday. I was a rookie police officer driving around, and I noticed a beautiful red Porsche in front of me. I ran the license plate and it came back as a stolen vehicle. I flicked on my flashing lights, but the Porsche took off at high speed. I chased it for ten or fifteen minutes, sometimes at one hundred miles per hour.

The suspect eventually crashed the car and ran off. We never found him. But I found something even more important.

The praise of my peers and supervisors. When I got back to the station, I was showered with compliments about how calmly I handled the radio while driving. I received a written commendation for my performance.

That taste of success affirmed my Vow to be seen in control. I ate it up. I became an adrenalin junkie and my peers cheered me on. Unfortunately, potential friends did not offer that kind of praise. They did not acknowledge my sacrifice serving the city. They only complained about their tickets. I sought only that which affirmed my Strategy of appearing in control and powerful.

I never gave one thought to how God protected me during that pursuit, and I never thanked God for the skills he gave me. My only thought was, "I want more of this." I was more determined than ever to make sure I appeared in control when any crisis occurred. Not because it was the right or excellent thing to do, but because it made me look good.

God's Purposes in Wounds

Although it is natural to want to avoid pain, and no one should seek to put themselves in harm's way, God's perspective is supernatural. It goes against every fiber of our being. Whether we are children or adults, it seems important to us to avoid Wounds and pain. But God offers a different perspective in the first chapter of the Epistle of James.

Pain from God's perspective should bring joy. Verse 2 tells us, "Count it all joy, my brothers, when you meet trials of various kinds." We recoil from such a concept. Being joyful about pain seems impossible. To do so will require us to trust God as never before, because we will be opening ourselves to potential hurt.

That can be done only as we surrender to whatever God knows will be for our best—even exposure to pain.

Pain produces change. Verses 3–4 tell us, "For you know that the testing of your faith produces steadfastness. And let steadfastness have its full effect, that you may be perfect and complete, lacking in nothing." Most of the changes in us come from testing.

Brad contacted us by email asking for our guidance. His wife was not willing to change. He felt completely beaten down by her. She criticized him and withheld sex. We replied, "Your self-image does not need to depend on the way your wife treats you. If it is, then she is your Idol because you look to her for your worth instead of to the Lord. You can actually have a godly self-image regardless of how horribly she treats you. The Lord wants you to look to him to see his value of you—to see who you are 'in Christ.'"

He told us he had heard such concepts before and appreciated them. But then he revealed his resistance by adding, "We would be happier if we were both trying to change."

Brad didn't really buy into the truth that God may have been allowing struggles and pain so that he would change, because we change the most in the midst of challenge. Quite possibly if both of them were happy, no spiritual growth would occur. We suspected that God wanted Brad to change regardless of his wife's lack of cooperation.

Pain brings wisdom. Verse 5 tells us, "If any of you lacks wisdom, let him ask God, who gives generously to all without reproach, and it will be given him." Pain most clearly reveals God's different, wise perspective.

The apostle Paul begged three times for relief from an unknown pain (many believe he had eye problems). Later he explained that God said to him, "My grace is sufficient for you, for my power is made perfect in weakness." So Paul concluded, "I will boast all the more gladly of my weaknesses, so that the power of Christ may rest upon me. For the sake of Christ, then, I am content with weaknesses, insults, hardships, persecutions, and calamities. For when I am weak, then I am strong" (2 Cor. 12:9–10).

Talk about a different perspective of gaining wisdom! Only when we surrender to God's plan can we see our childhood Wounds as part of his plan for us. Ministries such as Holding on to Hope Ministries help men who were sexually abused as children. That good work exists because its founder, Bill Harbeck, experienced that kind of pain. Wesley Stafford, president of Compassion International, has a heart for the wounded children of the world because he experienced physical and emotional pain as a child in a school for missionary children. The wisdom and motivation to fulfill God's purposes often come from the healing of our own hurts and Wounds.

Pain strips us of pride and control. James 1:6–8 tells us, "Let him ask in faith, with no doubting, for the one who doubts is like a wave of the sea that is driven and tossed by the wind. For that person must not suppose that he will receive anything from the Lord; he is a double-minded man, unstable in all his ways."

Faith requires dependence on God, because all of us are weak and prone to doubts. Humility says, "I don't have it all together. I need the Lord." With that attitude we can transition into a faith that says, "God, I trust in your way, and I acknowledge my double-minded ways of saying I trust you when my actions reveal that I don't."

Our faith can be strengthened when we review our childhood Wounds and are willing to be humbled by our weaknesses. Then we can identify how we formed Strategies to protect ourselves instead of trusting God.

When we want to avoid pain, we may be saying, "I must avoid pain because it will overwhelm me, and I won't be able to handle it. If I can't handle it, other people will see that I'm out of control and inadequate. I must prevent this from happening."

But pain can be an opportunity to force us to cling to God. It can help us to see our double-minded, unstable ways and to recognize that we must surrender ourselves totally to God because we can no longer provide for ourselves. Then God promises us his strength while we feel the pain of our childhood Wounds.

Pain reminds us of the hope of heaven. Verses 9–12 assure us,

> Let the lowly brother boast in his exaltation, and
> the rich in his humiliation, because like a flower of
> the grass he will pass away. For the sun rises with its
> scorching heat and withers the grass; its flower falls,
> and its beauty perishes. So also will the rich man fade
> away in the midst of his pursuits. Blessed is the man
> who remains steadfast under trial, for when he has
> stood the test he will receive the crown of life, which
> God has promised to those who love him.

Remembering the pain of our Wounds reminds us that this earth is not our final destination. Riches or poverty, Wounds or joy, accomplishment or failure will fade away. Though life is as fleeting as a withering blade of grass, one day we will receive the crown of life and be set free from every shred of pain. The glory, joy, and delight of rejoicing in our Savior will cause all the memories about the pain of earth to fade away.

And though it is hard to conceive of it now, our response toward the pain of earth will be what Isaiah described in 28:27–29:

> *Dill is not threshed with a threshing sledge,*
> *   nor is a cart wheel rolled over cumin,*
> *but dill is beaten out with a stick,*
> *   and cumin with a rod.*
> *Does one crush grain for bread?*
> *   No, he does not thresh it forever;*
> *when he drives his cart wheel over it*
> *   with his horses, he does not crush it.*
> *This also comes from the* LORD *of hosts;*
> *   he is wonderful in counsel*
> and excellent in wisdom.

In eternity we will acknowledge that God "broke us" gently, not more than was appropriate. He did not crush us unnecessarily or without a godly design. He only allowed the pain that would mold us and fashion us into something useful for his intentions.

God will not allow pain to destroy us. He lets us suffer only what will draw us closer to his wise, loving heart for the purposes of creating something that will nourish others and bring him glory. We tend to think he should spare us from pain, but if he did, we would not need him, nor would we long for heaven.

Sharon knows these truths. She was verbally and physically abused. Though members of her family knew what was going on, they did not protect her. Her only defense was hiding in the closet when her mother's temper began to flare. She always wondered why her mother never found her there.

When Sharon was an adult, she joined a small group where God began to heal her. At one of the meetings, she shared another layer of her pain and a remaining shard of anger toward God. As she was telling her story, she felt as if she were twelve years old again and felt the same fear she had experienced when her mother was searching for her. One of the members of the group welcomed Sharon into her arms, and she hid there for at least ten minutes, reliving the pain and fear.

As she usually did, she cried out to God, "God, why didn't you stop the hurt?"

Then, still in the safety of her friend's arms, her question turned to, "God, do you love me?"

In that moment, God took her back to the closet, and for the first time she knew she was not alone. Jesus had been there with her and had prevented her mom from finding her. He had always been there, but she couldn't trust him enough then to crawl into his arms.

Sharon explains, "But then as I felt the safety of my friend's arms, I could allow God to wrap his arms around me. Emotionally, I was the little girl snuggling against him. I told God I was sorry I wouldn't go into his arms in the closet but that I wanted to now.

"As I waited, I saw in my mind a picture of me in his lap being wrapped in his arms and held by his bleeding, nail-pierced hands. He held me tightly against his side bleeding from the spear wound. Surprisingly, I was not put off by the blood; instead I wanted it to cover me. I saw the love of Jesus who suffered for me and with me. I felt quiet and at rest. My anger was gone. I no longer needed to try to protect myself. My tears became tears of surrender rather than anger.

"I know now that earth can never meet my needs, but the love of Jesus is more than sufficient. I'll always be hurt on this earth, but some day I'll be with Jesus without any pain at all."

Reflections and Group Discussion Questions

1. What emotion surfaced from this chapter? Why?

2. Look back at your answers to the questions at the end of Chapter One. What did you answer for the question, "What would you like to avoid at all costs?" In light of this chapter, can you identify a Wound that might have created that commitment?

3. Now look at your answer to the question, "Who has hurt you the most?" In light of this chapter, what is your reaction to your answer? Do you want to change your answer to someone else? How do you feel about that person now?

4. Could you share one of the Wounds from your past with the group?

5. At the time of the Wounding, how did you try to protect yourself?

6. What purpose(s) do you think God had in allowing your Wound(s)?

7. Is there any concept from this chapter that you disagree with? Why?

8. Has this chapter influenced you in some way? Explain.

9. As you think of the Wounds from your past, what is God saying to you right now?

10. Which Scripture verse from this chapter was most meaningful for you?

Chapter 4

The Message

We are meaning-makers, hard wired to interpret life.

—Paul David Tripp

It's not our raw experiences that determine our lives but the meaning we make of them— the stories we tell and the stories we believe.

—Mike Wilkerson

As we saw in our last chapter, bad things happen to everyone, and when we are children, we don't have the maturity or knowledge to interpret correctly the things people do and say. Hopefully, someone will help us. But so often the adults around us are not even aware of our distress or our wrong perceptions. To them what happens may seem insignificant, or they may feel helpless to intervene. Plus children can interpret the same incident differently.

Children do also hear accurate Messages. But every child, no matter how well-loved and well-guided, experiences misperceptions and learns to manage his or her life without God's control. This is what the Bible calls the mind of the "natural person." "The natural person does not accept the things of the

Spirit of God, for they are folly to him, and he is not able to understand them because they are spiritually discerned" (1 Cor. 2:14). This "natural person" residing within us from childhood is created both by the sin nature and by our early experiences. But there is hope. Just two verses later Paul writes that the Christian has "the mind of Christ."

We do not come to know the full measure of that "mind of Christ" instantly at conversion. In order to grow in that under-standing we must identify the "natural person's" Messages we have believed from the beginning. Some of these are obvious. One man told us, for example, "My mother always said I wouldn't amount to anything." But there are also subtle ones that affect us.

Linda's foundational Wounds that later contributed to her anorexia occurred every time she handed her elementary school report card to her father. He would always respond, "How did Kelly do on her report card?" Kelly was Linda's best friend.

His question sent her a message: "I'm not as important as Kelly." Linda decided she needed to get straight A's in order to keep his focus on her. This fed her Strategy to be perfect, which in turn fueled her anorexia. Of course, many other things happened as she was growing up, but she gave this example as a starting point for her attempts to figure out life on her own.

During her healing process as an adult, Linda told her father about the Message she had received. He was horrified and explained, "I'm so sorry. I knew Kelly didn't have a loving family, and I was concerned about her. But I never intended to communicate that you aren't important. Please forgive me."

Messages are Satan's lies. He always suggests that God doesn't deserve our trust because he doesn't want the best for us. No wonder the apostle Paul admonishes us in Ephesians 6:16 about the armor of God, saying, "In all circumstances take up the shield of faith, with which you can extinguish all the flaming darts of the evil one." The flaming darts are these Messages that form the foundation of our belief system and create Sinful Strategies. Faith in God's good love and gracious gift will reject these satanic Messages.

Remember our model? Wounds create Messages, which foster Wrong Beliefs/Distorted Images, which conceive Vows, which birth Sinful Strategies. These Strategies make us distrust God. When our Strategy is threatened, we get Hooked. As a result, we reject the power the Spirit offers and we react in opposition to the fruit of the Spirit. But we can come to the point of Repenting from these Strategies and Surrendering to greater trust in God through a Process of Growth. That is the journey we are on in this book.

What Are These Messages Like?

Our Enemy, Satan, can be either obvious or subtle in fashioning and throwing these darts of lies at us. Here are some examples:

Brody was a sickly child with real illnesses, yet his stepfather constantly told him, "Just try harder to get better." That "just try harder" Message affects him today. He has little compassion for himself or for anyone else who is sick. He is a workaholic, and his family therefore feels slighted and unimportant. Brody views God as a taskmaster who requires perfection.

Jenny's grandmother cared for her while Jenny's mom worked at home typing mailing labels. Whenever Jenny approached her mom, her grandmother stopped her and said, "Don't bother your mom now; she's doing something important." The Message Jenny "heard" was, "You're not important enough for your mother." As an adult, she believes she's not important enough to bother God with her prayers.

When Mason's father left, his parting words to eight-year-old Mason were, "Don't cry. You're the man of the house now." This message of "men don't cry—be in control" has affected him his whole life. Feeling emotionally connected with a woman scares him because he feels out of control. Mason views God as an unemotional Being with little compassion or empathy.

Those are only a sampling of possibilities. Unfortunately, there are more. These Messages can be grouped into three general categories:

- Wrong Beliefs about Life
- Wrong Beliefs about God
- Distorted Images about Self.

Here are some samples of each that don't even begin to include all the possibilities in Satan's quiver of flaming arrows.

Wrong Beliefs about Life:
- People can't be trusted.
- Life is always waiting to throw you a curve.
- There's no hope; why even try.
- Worry prevents bad things from occurring.

Wrong Beliefs about God:
- God is only interested in the "big" things.
- God doesn't care about me.
- God is waiting for me to mess up.
- Prayer doesn't do any good.

Distorted Images about Self:
- I'm worthless.
- I'm a failure.

- I'm invisible.
- I'm stupid.
- I could have done better.
- I'm on my own.

What Biblical Instruction Don't You Like?

One way we can identify the Messages caused by our Wounds is through the answers to the questions in Chapter One. For this particular chapter, look at your answer to the question, "What instruction in the Bible do you have trouble obeying or understanding?" Did you wonder why we asked this? It is because your answer to this question could indicate the wrong Message(s) you believe. Let's look at the examples from the beginning of this chapter.

Brody, who believes he was sick because he didn't try hard enough, would answer this question with Psalm 46:10: "Be still, and know that I am God." He just doesn't understand the concept of relaxing in the Lord. His father said to just keep trying and that would heal him.

Jenny, who believes she is not important because her mother did not have time for her, gave this verse: "The LORD your God is in your midst, a mighty one who will save; he will rejoice over you with gladness; he will quiet you by his love; he will exult over you with loud singing" (Zeph. 3:17). She laughs in embarrassment to think God could rejoice over her. After all, her mom didn't.

Mason, who defines a true man as one devoid of emotion, discounts John 11:35, "Jesus wept." When the topic of Jesus' humanity comes up, he will argue, "Well, that's the only time the Word says Jesus cried. So, obviously, it was an anomaly."

What Scripture did you write down when you answered that question? Pay attention to the Scriptures that you don't like or that you struggle to obey. They may indicate a Wrong Belief about life or about God, or a Distorted Image about yourself that is blocking you from trusting God and obeying him.

Formulas Reveal Messages

By formulas, we mean the plans or ideas we set in concrete and tell God, "Don't ask me to change, and don't lead me in a different way." They prevent us from abiding in the Vine. God didn't give Abraham a map; he just said, "Leave now, and I'll show you where to go."

But I (Kathy) want a detailed map. Some time ago I was questioning God about how to respond to a rocky and hurtful relationship. It seemed as if God was inspiring a plan through a book I was reading. I believed I knew God's will, and it included lots of boundaries and little grace. I was convinced that my friend must follow my guidelines in order to have a friendship with me.

Then my spiritual eyes were opened. I saw the formula I was creating, a formula designed to protect me from my childhood Message that I was inferior. My road map with my current friend built a wall protecting me from rejection and feeling inferior.

The Holy Spirit invited me to take this situation "captive to obey Christ" (2 Cor. 10:5). He whispered, "What would it be like to trust me moment by moment as you interact with your friend, whom I love?" I realized I was not abiding in trust in God. I was fashioning a Self-Protective Sinful Strategy that left out God. So I repented of my sin and surrendered to however God might lead.

As a result of those Wounds that I (Larry) received in junior and senior high school, I believed Satan's lies that I was alone and on my own. No one could protect me, so I would care for myself. I never wondered if God was inviting me to include him. I had a formula that worked well to keep me in some semblance of control. I approached most things in life expecting the worst and preparing for it. I mentally rehearsed options that would keep me physically safe and emotionally distant. My police training sharpened my cynical views. Even on the most routine calls I would mentally note hiding places for ambushes, evaluate the depth of a kill zone, and look for safe escape and evasion routes. Every situation could be my last, so I approached all of life with caution. Even when I was not on duty, I prepared for the worse, never asking God for his opinion or direction.

I now look back and see that my formula worked as a cover for my poor choices. I would envision how some family outing might get complicated or impinge on my plans for the next week. If Kathy wanted to take the kids to the park within two days, I could come up with some sort of excuse not to go. I felt inadequate as a father, so I used the formula of negativity to prevent being exposed to possible failure. Just as rose-colored glasses might brighten someone's outlook, I used gray-tinged glasses of cynicism and emotional distance to help make choices against relationships that might not work as I hoped.

Yes, God sometimes directs us to set boundaries, make plans, create a mission statement, and establish goals. Jesus himself set up guidelines and boundaries for being in contact with others. He removed himself when appropriate (Luke 5:15–16), and he didn't do everything other people wanted him to. He constantly abided in the Father and only followed his Father's leading. Therefore, you and I need to ask whether our plans are truly God's leading or whether we are responding to ungodly Messages that leave out God.

The Christian community loves "boundaries" so much that it almost seems heretical to suggest that setting boundaries could be a way to tell God to "buzz off!" When we set boundaries, though, we could leave little room for God's intervention or his invitation to change course. Hopefully, our attitude is, "Lord, this is the boundary I trust you are directing me to set, but I am open to any changes you communicate in the future."

The difficulty is that each of us assumes our particular belief is that kind of formula—one right from God's mind. But as we have seen, our choices can be affected by our Wounds and the Messages from them—and we don't even know it.

So what Messages are revealed by formulas?

Now we want to be clear. We are not encouraging anyone to put themselves in a place of temptation, but we must ask ourselves: are we trusting in God, or are we trusting in our formula?

We counseled Sam, who set a boundary for himself that he could play basketball only one hour a day. He explained that he so loved shooting hoops that he could easily do too much of it and fail to spend time with God in prayer and Bible study.

As a guy who has always enjoyed sports, I asked him, "What does playing basketball do for you?"

"I love the feeling of getting better and the recognition of others because I really am good at it. It feels like a little reward every time that ball swishes through the hoop. So, you see, that's why I personally need to set boundaries for it. It has been an Idol in the past."

"What would it be like to let God direct you in how much time you play?"

He looked surprised and paused. "Well, if I were to ask God each day what he wanted me to do, it would all work out—but that's only if I could do it perfectly. But I know myself. Believe me, I'm not perfect! Instead I'll let my natural weaknesses kick in and take control. That's why I need this boundary. Does that make sense?"

"Well, let's see. I hear you saying that you aren't allowed to fail. That you must depend upon your formula to prevent growth that could come by needing to ask for forgiveness. Have you ever thought how even failure can bring growth through Repentance and Surrender? How would that Process of Growth bring greater dependence upon God?"

Sam sputtered in shock. His Adam's apple bobbed as he swallowed his emotion. Finally he spoke. "I can't even fail once for fear God won't be pleased with me—and then reject me. That's the Message I've believed all my life. As a child, my father never was pleased with anything I did. And if I disobeyed him, he would ignore me for days at a time. I can see now that if I depended upon God for how much time I play basketball and yet went beyond that, I could accept his forgiveness. Then I could ask him to teach me to make him as fulfilling to me as sports."

Sam smiled even as he brushed away a tear. "What an exciting thought to think of an opportunity to depend upon God more and to experience his forgiving grace when I fail."

The next time I saw Sam, he told me, "I didn't follow God's leading perfectly, yet I didn't sense that God was ignoring me. I asked him to forgive me, and he cleansed me. I was encouraged to continue to ask God to empower me to obey as he directed me. I think that false Message is diminishing."

God had begun the healing in Sam's heart. He is no longer held captive by the lie: "I'm only accepted if I perform perfectly."

Does any formula hold you captive? How does it prevent you from growing in trust in God?

The Message Creates Sin Management

We drove over to our favorite fast food restaurant for lunch. As we neared the parking lot, we were grateful to see that the potholes had been filled in. The asphalt was nice and black. Then we drove in and bumped along much as before. Only black tar had been poured atop the asphalt.

Immediately I said, "That's what Sin Management is like, Kathy. We just cover over the potholes and it looks good; but there really hasn't been any deep change in our lives."

When we believe incorrect and ungodly Messages, we seek to cover over our unholiness with Sin Management. We force ourselves to do the right thing when we want to look good, but our hearts haven't been impacted. It's like raising our voice to our child, but when the phone rings, we immediately calm down and sweetly say hello. We force ourselves to be good, but we are not motivated by the Holy Spirit. God doesn't want Sin Management. He wants obedience and worship from the heart.

Adam and Eve were really good at Sin Management. They covered the evidence of believing Satan's Message with fig leaves instead of asking God to heal their sin-sick hearts. In our shame from the Messages, we try to cover up our neediness instead of seeking Repentance leading to cleansing and the Spirit's empowerment.

Sin Management results from not fully facing sin and taking responsibility. Micah 2:6–7 gives God's perspective:

"Do not preach"—thus they preach—
    "one should not preach of such things;
    disgrace will not overtake us."
Should this be said, O house of Jacob?
    Has the LORD grown impatient?

> Are these his deeds?
> Do not my words do good
>   to him who walks uprightly?

The false prophets say to Micah and other godly prophets like Isaiah: "Do not talk about judgment. God and his Spirit don't work that way. He is a God of love; he won't bring judgment. Do not tell us what we do wrong; only tell us what we're doing right. Don't talk about sin; only talk about happiness. Do not call us to holiness; let us continue to do what meets our needs."

Elyse Fitzpatrick writes in *Idols of the Heart*:

> Instead of just trying to control my temper when I'm
> criticized, for instance, I need to understand that
> the reason I'm angry is because I crave and worship
> other people's opinions of me. I need to repent of my
> thoughts about myself and agree with God that only
> He is worthy of praise (at the same time that I repent
> of my sinful anger).

Sin Management is when we are trying to get our needs met without looking for the underlying cause. And we come up with many creative ways to do it.

- We cry out to God, "Just take away my emotional pain; don't point out the sin that causes it."
- We cry out to other people: "Don't look at what I lack; just pay attention to where I succeed."
- We cry out to God: "I've learned my lesson; now remove this trial."
- We claim, "Good things are happening to me; I'm blessed by God."

That last one may be a surprise. We base our spirituality upon our performance or our success, instead of the condition of our heart. Author and pastor Paul Tripp recognized that struggle within his own ministry. After exciting successes in his church, he wrote,

> God did not act because he endorsed my manner of living, but because of his zeal for his own glory and his faithfulness to his promises of grace for his people. God has the authority and power to use whatever instruments he chooses in whatever way he chooses. Ministry success is always more a statement about God than about the people he uses for his purpose. I had it all wrong. I took credit that I did not deserve for what I could not do. I made it about me, so I didn't see myself as headed for disaster and in deep need for the rescue of God's grace. I was a man in need of rescuing grace.

Of course, none of us will obey perfectly and, indeed, obedience is a matter of choosing God's way. But Sin Management is obedience on the surface and not from motives that desire God's glory.

What to Do with the Message

So what do we do with the Message? As you will see in our next chapter, if we do not correct the Message, it becomes a Vow. As a child, we respond to the Message with a Vow in order to protect ourselves—because we don't know any better.

But as Christian adults, we have a choice. We can identify the Message and rebuke it as 2 Corinthians 10:5 tells us. Remember that verse? "We destroy arguments and every lofty opinion raised against the knowledge of God, and take every thought captive to obey Christ."

In the last chapter I shared with you the Message I received when the water polo coach almost drowned me. Actually, I got two Messages: I am powerless. I am less of a man. Looking back, I can sort through them more clearly.

- The first Message was true, but I denied it.
- The second Message was false, but I believed it.

My first thought—I am powerless—is actually true. I was powerless then, and I am powerless now. I am without the power of the Holy Spirit, that is! Judah's King Jehoshaphat had the right idea when he prayed, "O our God, will you not execute judgment on them? For we are powerless against this great horde that is coming against us. We do not know what to do, but our eyes are on you" (2 Chron. 20:12).

As Jehoshaphat knew, only God is powerful. Circumstances and the brokenness in this world remind me on a daily basis that apart from God, I have no power. The godly reaction to facing my weakness should drive me to my knees in trust and need of him. But the inclination of my heart, apart from Christ, is to deny this truth and strike out on my own to make sure I'm safe. Surrender to such a Sovereign oftentimes is just too frightening for the rebellious heart. It's too dangerous to trust God because he cannot be controlled.

The second thought—I am less of a man—is false. What happens to me does not diminish my manhood. That is a status given by God because I am made in his image. Satan tried to make me agree with that lie and, unfortunately, I cooperated.

But today I agree with the truth and reject the falsehood.

Satan is clever in that he mixes the truth with the lies. When he assails us with reminders of childhood Messages and even invents new ones to throw at us as adults, we do have a choice. We can pay attention to the thoughts coming into our minds and evaluate them against the truths of God's Word.

Picture it like this. Satan's flaming missiles (Eph. 6:16) fly toward us. They may be a mixture of truth and lies. They may look completely reasonable. But we must seize them as if we were grabbing an arrow, evaluate each one, and ask, "Is this the truth? Does this line up with the Word of God?" If the arrow is a lie, we can cast it from us, but if it is the truth, we can allow the arrow to continue its journey into our hearts and minds. It is a constant battle to be alert to the false Messages about God, life, and ourselves. Thankfully God wants to empower us.

Reflections and Group Discussion Questions

1. Give at least one example of a false Message from your childhood for each category.
   God:
   Life:
   Self:

2. Have you ever had an opportunity to discuss with a sibling your Messages about a shared childhood experience? What insights did you gain?

3. What is your reaction to the principle in 2 Corinthians 10:5: "Take every thought captive to obey Christ"? Do you find this difficult or easy to do?

4. Give an example of applying 2 Corinthians 10:5.

5. What Message diminishes your trust in God?

6. What was your reaction to your answer for question 7 (from Chapter One) about a Scripture you find hard to obey or understand? How did it reveal one of your Messages?

7. Which story in this chapter do you relate to the most?

8. Can you identify a formula that connects to a child-hood Message?

9. What was your reaction to the concept of Sin Management? Can you isolate any elements of that in you?

10. Memorize 2 Corinthians 10:5.

Chapter 5

The Vow

*Idols aren't just stone statues. No, idols are the thoughts,
desires, longings, and expectations that we worship
in the place of the true God. Idols cause us to ignore
the true God in search of what we think we need.*

—Elyse Fitzpatrick

*Keep in mind that the root of ugly emotion
does not lie in how others have treated you, but
rather in your demand that they treat you well.*

—Larry Crabb

Have you ever said phrases like these? How did you complete the phrase?

- I vowed . . .
- I decided . . .
- I concluded . . .
- I believed . . .
- I'll make sure . . .
- I'm committed to . . .
- I'm never going to . . .
- I'll always . . .

If you have—and we all have—you may have made a Vow. The different kinds of Vows are numerous. They erupt within us in order to protect us from the pain of a Wound and its corresponding Message.

Remember our model?

The Wound creates a Message (giving birth to Wrong Beliefs and Distorted Images) resulting in a Vow, creating a Sinful Strategy, causing us to become Hooked.

Ultimately we can fight the Vows through Repentance and Surrender while we are in a Process of Growth. But when we are not aware of the Vows we have chosen, we become Hooked and wonder why.

We may be aware of what a Vow is—a voluntary commitment to act, be, or do—or *not* to act, be, or do. But what might not be so apparent are the ways a Message prompts a Vow. The Vow is our response to prevent another incidence of the pain inflicted by the original Message. Or, as we mentioned previously, even good events can create a Message. In that case, Vows spring from the desire to continue receiving whatever life-giving Message the experience seemed to offer.

Here are some additional examples of Vows. Try to imagine what kind of Wound and Message might have been at the core of these Vows:

- I will never be sick.
- I won't cry.
- I will make sure you come through for me.
- I will be capable.
- I'll never be vulnerable again.
- I refuse to be seen as lazy.
- No one will treat me like that again.

- I must use every opportunity to serve God.
- When I'm a parent, I won't treat my children the way I'm being treated.
- I'll make sure no one fails me again.

I remember a girlhood experience that strengthened my Vow to not express my desires. Growing up, I loved my bachelor uncle's individual attention, which did not occur often.

One time, though, Uncle Frank and my father included me on a trip with them to go visit their sister, who lived several hours away. As I rode in the backseat by myself, I thought, *It would be so much fun to sit by Uncle Frank.* My eight-year-old heart longed for his attention.

But wounds from the past made me hesitant to express my desires. My desire seemed selfish, so I felt voiceless and powerless. Besides, if the wish wasn't granted, what would that say about my worth and value? Finally, after agonizing about it, I talked myself into asking, "Um, Daddy, could I sit up front with you and Uncle Frank?"

Uncle Frank said, "Wonderful! I'd like to lie down in the backseat and take a nap."

After switching places, I sat staring out the window into the dark, afraid to brush away my tears. I didn't want my father to see my disappointment. I quickly concluded, "See? It doesn't do any good to ask. Don't even try."

That Vow was a defensive measure to avoid the pain of hearing the Message: "You must not be important enough because they didn't surmise the desire of your heart." My young heart thought they should know what I wanted.

This experience along with others solidified my Vow: "I'm never going to ask, because it doesn't do any good, and it proves my unimportance."

Are Vows Affecting You?

It is not always clear how Vows arise out of distrust in God and how they bring disappointment in life and ungodly reactions toward other people.

When I was still a boy in high school, my father had left the church and joined a non-Christian cult. He literally spent four or five hours every day studying the Bible. After a few years he could spout Scripture with the best preachers I knew of. But in my heart I knew his interpretations and applications were heresy.

A couple of times I tried to debate him, but I could never make any headway. My dad would get highly animated and intense, completely disregarding anyone else's opinions. Quite frankly, he again felt unsafe to me, similar to the time he threw my toy fire engine into my room (Chapter Three). I consciously moved to a state of peaceful coexistence and never brought up biblical issues with him again.

However, this peaceful coexistence was broken one day when Kathy asked my father a question about his faith, with the intent of trying to show him love. This launched him on another endless monologue. Kathy looked over to me for help, but I wouldn't even look at her. She knew I had checked out and she was on her own. Later that night I angrily told Kathy never to engage my father in such a discussion again. She later told me that the tone of my anger made her shrink emotionally.

Looking back today, I can see how those Vows of self-protection I made as a child harmed the most loving and important relationship I had on earth—with Kathy. I now know my father needed to be proven right because his new "faith" demanded it to qualify for salvation. My Vow to be in control, especially around someone who did not seem safe, created my withdrawal. I didn't want to be proven unknowledgeable and thus vulnerable to criticism. My Vow damaged our marriage.

Examples from Scripture

God takes vows seriously. In Numbers 30:2, God commands that if we make a vow, we should keep it. But the kind of Vows we're talking about are part of the "old person" based in distrust of God. We should repent of them and trust in God instead. The Tower of Babel is a good example of sinful Vows.

The tower builders said, "Come, let us build ourselves a city and a tower with its top in the heavens, and let us make a name for ourselves, lest we be dispersed over the face of the whole earth" (Gen. 11:4). Do you hear the Vow? "We Vow that no one will scatter us abroad. Therefore we will make ourselves a name by building a city and a tower. Other people will be impressed and not scatter us or forget us. We're in control."

They were lapping at the cistern of their own making and drinking mud. That is definitely a Vow God did not want kept, so he scattered them—in spite of their best efforts.

Similarly, James 4:13 warns against the wrong kind of Vow: "Come now, you who say, 'Today or tomorrow we will go into such and such a town and spend a year there and trade and make a profit.'" No doubt James heard from the people things such as, "I vow to make a profit from my company." "I'm going to make sure I'm successful." "I'll never be a failure like so-and-so." "I will be in control of my future." God is left out because of a lack of trust in his goodness and his lordship.

Even committed Christians can make a Vow. We read an interview with a prominent pastor who said at the beginning of his ministry that he would stay twenty-five years in his church and then do something else. That number of years has passed, so now he is retiring. There was no mention that he was led by God. He had determined what would happen.

In contrast, James gives the right perspective: "Instead you ought to say, 'If the Lord wills, we will live and do this or that.' As it is, you boast in your arrogance. All such boasting is evil" (4:15–16).

Unfortunately, most of us are not taught as children to watch for the formation of sinful Vows that result from Wounds and Messages. How can we identify those Vows from childhood (and even adulthood) so that we can prevent being Hooked?

Demands Reveal Vows

Vows can be expressed in our daily living as a "demand." The influences of Demands are unseen because they are such an entrenched part of our thinking. We've always believed "that way." There is no other way of thinking or doing.

This was true for the apostle Peter in Acts 10. Peter had vowed never to eat unclean food and had been totally obedient. And we would not be surprised if he gloried in his obedience. He knew he was following God's rules, and this made him righteous in God's eyes. But God told him to do the thing he had Vowed never to do, and he reacted in sin.

> But Peter said, "By no means, Lord; for I have never eaten anything that is common or unclean." And the voice came to him again a second time, "What God has made clean, do not call common." This happened

three times, and the thing was taken up at once to
heaven (verses 14–16).

Imagine that! Peter made a Vow and then demanded that God
support his Vow. Everything was either clean or unclean, and
that included people—Jews and Gentiles. God knew that if
Peter's Vow remained, it would prevent Peter from participat-
ing in God's next opportunity to minister. Because Cornelius,
a Gentile, was about to summon Peter, and without a major
change in Peter's worldview, God's plan for launching Christian
ministry to the whole world would be squelched.

Peter was lapping at the cistern of his own righteousness, and he was not even aware of it. This is what Vows do to
us. We argue with God because we believe we are right. We
demand that the world—and even God—submit to our limited
understanding.

Let's consider some other ways that Demands reveal Vows.

- If I vow that no one will ever hurt me again, I'll
  demand that people be perfect. (God may want to
  use even hurt for our good and his glory.)
- If I vow that I'll never treat my children like I was
  treated, I demand perfection from myself. (God
  doesn't expect me to be perfect; otherwise I am
  thinking I'm equal with God.)
- If I vow that I'll never be sick, I demand that no one
  ever comes around me with any illness. (Living in
  this world exposes us to illness wherever we are.)
- If I vow that my spouse is responsible to meet my
  needs, I'll demand that he/she never disappoint me.
  (Only God can truly meet our needs and never disappoint us.)

Can you identify any Demand in your life and then see how it was birthed in a Vow?

Disappointments and Hurts Reveal Vows

Demands and Vows often dress themselves in the term "supposed to."

Samantha knows that expression. She would never think of herself as being "demanding," but her Vows and Demands fuel her sinful responses to her husband. She told us, "I'm furious because I followed my husband to this new area. I trusted that he would take care of me. A woman is supposed to feel secure and taken care of."

Her anger is her way of demanding that her husband perform to her expectations. After we heard her childhood memories of being mocked because of her weight, we could easily identify the Message of "I'm not important" and her protective Vow, "I must be cared for in order to prove I'm important and valuable."

When we suggested to her that only God can provide the security and care she hungered for, she bristled, "Then why did I get married?" Samantha was unable to move past her hurt and come to the point of Repentance and Surrender.

Pay attention to what you demand of others and yourself, even of God, and those Demands may point to the Vows you have made.

Disappointments and Hurts Can Be Avoided

All of us have felt disappointed. It's that feeling that what we expected, desired, or felt entitled to was not fulfilled. We have said, in effect, to some person or thing, "Here's my heart. You must come through for me; otherwise, I will feel: (pick one/

many) worthless, ignored, embarrassed, abandoned—and I have vowed never to feel like that! And that means I'm entitled to get angry or withdraw in order to protect my heart."

We see other people or things as our "living water" when they are actually broken cisterns from which we are slurping the muddy water of disappointment and hurt. Then we become Hooked and choose anger, depression, withdrawal, bitterness, resentment, a critical spirit, or worry.

But look at Jesus' perspective in John 2:24–25: "Jesus on his part did not entrust himself to them, because he knew all people and needed no one to bear witness about man, for he himself knew what was in man."

Although these verses primarily talk about Jesus' physical being, Jesus didn't depend upon anyone to define him or to label him. He could stay strong because he knew realistically who men were. As a result, he was never disappointed by them. He knew men would fail him; only his Father would never let him down. So he based his expectations solely on the Father.

In contrast, we expect people never to fail us. No wonder we are disappointed. We believe that if we will just communicate our needs clearly, other people will feel motivated to meet them.

Granted, the word "disappointed" could mean something not sinful—something like, "My expectations weren't met, but it doesn't bother me. I'm just identifying something that didn't happen." This is possible—but only when we don't set our heart on it. And that is difficult to do.

But because we have God's power to live supernaturally, we *can* have a different perspective. Just think of the joy and freedom that would result!

Entitlements Reveal Vows

At a conference years ago, we talked casually to a man who said something like, "To me, it's annoying and discouraging to do all the 'right' things caring for my body and it still doesn't function right."

Of course, he had no idea he had just stated an Entitlement. An Entitlement is something that I believe I have a right to, or it may be a guarantee of access to something. A right is itself an Entitlement. Our new friend presumed that he knew what God wanted for him, which is the first step toward having an Entitlement, and then he demanded that it be the way he expected. In his mind, he did things right and, therefore, he was entitled to reap his anticipated rewards. But what a burden we assume when we try to be God of our own lives.

As Christians we have no rights and Entitlements. We can only rightfully claim the promise of our inheritances in Christ and any other promises made in Scripture. How deceived our minds and hearts can become in this area of thinking.

Kathy can testify that on more than one occasion I have experienced a deceived heart while driving. I have become angry when someone went too slow, cut me off, or seemed so clueless that they momentarily ruined my day. At times, I have even found an inappropriate adjective easily popping from my tongue to describe a character flaw in that driver—some insult that does not reflect the image-bearing status of the offender.

Being so easily Hooked began to trouble me. After all, I didn't know that person. I knew their behavior really said nothing about me, so I was vexed by my angry outbursts that seemed to come from nowhere. "What can be underneath this anger?" I wondered. "Why do I have so much trouble checking these erupting feelings that prevent the fruit of the Spirit from flowing through me?"

So I started examining my heart. During this time, Kathy and I went on our first overseas ministry trip to Caracas, Venezuela. Traffic was so congested there. During the day it was always bumper to bumper. If there were two lanes of traffic in one direction, the drivers would make it three. I learned you must stop for certain red lights, but others you never stop for because you will get rear-ended.

In all this crazy driving, I never saw another driver get angry. Everyone moved in real close and honked their horns just to alert their driving "neighbor" that they were there. It was clear that no one had the expectation that they had personal space. The entire street was fair game for any driver. Everyone just honked their way around town in what seemed like a chaotic order that made sense to them. They drove like madmen without the "mad."

We know the American highway system is vastly different. We expect, no, we demand our personal space. Let's face it. Many of us are totally self-centered while we drive.

As I reflected on the root causes of my anger, the Lord showed me that something darker was hiding beneath my anger. Comparing the driving culture of third-world countries and ours gave me a glimpse of what really was going on in my heart. I expected self-fulfillment with no obstacles because I felt I was worthy and entitled to receive such good treatment. I was Hooked because I possessed an Entitlement attitude fueled by my childhood Vow to always remain in control.

When drivers bothered me, it felt to me like I was losing control. That other driver was in control, and that was unacceptable.

Therefore, I could call them names, because they obviously did not recognize my value.

I was convicted when I realized that my anger was grounded in a sense of Entitlement. As an act of suitable Repentance, the Lord led me to share this revelation with a men's Bible study I was leading. I remember saying, "In my selfish hubris, I kind of expected all the other drivers to get out of my way and yield to my right to drive the highways unrestricted."

It was an ugly revelation. I confessed to them how I repented of my pride. It was clear I did not have an anger problem. I had a self-inflated-me problem. I was shocked and embarrassed with my high opinion of myself.

I can honestly say that I was unaware of this unredeemed area of my heart until I started examining why I became Hooked while driving and recognized the Vow that was the foundation for it. I was surprised when I saw how the smoke of my anger was merely evidence of the burning fire of pride and presumption in rebellion to Christ.

After I visited God's living spring, I found myself less stressed in driving. I stopped getting Hooked by other drivers (at least, not so often and not so volcanically), and I found myself giving grace to drivers who made mistakes. My pace in life is slower by choice now. Entitlement is a pernicious belief that drives us to expect we can get life on our terms. It leaves God out of the picture.

What do you feel you are entitled to? What are you counting on for fulfillment? What are you afraid God will not provide? What if he said "drink from me only"? Could your Entitlement of choice reveal a Vow?

Vows Create Idols

One Christmas when Audrey (Larry's mom) still lived with us, our then-three-year-old grandson, Raffi, was fascinated by Audrey's walker. He loved to push it around. When he walked (or ran) away with it, Audrey became visibly anxious. Fear was written all over her face. She called out to him, "Don't take away my walker. I need it. I depend on it. I'm just an old woman, so don't hurt it."

Initially, I was miffed (another denial word for angry) that Audrey would think we wouldn't provide well for her. My Vow to be considered dependable and capable got Hooked. But I also felt sad to think that Audrey believed she was on her own. She had to fuss at Raf and try to control something she had no control over since she didn't have the strength to retrieve the walker herself or to follow him to supervise what he did with it. We, on the other hand, could do something about it, and we did. We decided that Raf couldn't play with it because his doing so caused her too much anxiety.

Each of us has our kind of "walker" that we believe we need. Whether it is security, peace, a relationship, a plan, a desire, a reputation . . . pick which "walker" you believe you need for your security and happiness. This becomes our Idol because we are demanding that it provide for us what only God can provide. We expect it to protect us in ways that only God can.

An Idol indicates we are not trusting God to provide or protect what we need, even though Philippians 4:19 promises that God will meet all our true needs. Instead, we believe we are on our own and call out to the offending party who is threatening what we think we need: "Don't take away my walker. I need it. I'm dependent on it. I'm just a helpless Christian, so don't hurt it."

The Lord thankfully is not miffed, but he *is* standing by with godly sorrow saying, "I'll take care of you. I promise that I will provide everything you need and protect you according to my good plan. Trust me."

What is your "walker"? What have you vowed you must have? How have you vowed you will never be seen? What are you fearful someone will take away or expose? Whatever you feel tense or anxious about, that is your Idol which has emerged from a Vow.

Consider Isaiah 46:1-2:

Bel bows down; Nebo stoops;
    their idols are on beasts and livestock;
these things you carry are borne
    as burdens on weary beasts.
They stoop; they bow down together;
    they cannot save the burden,
    but themselves go into captivity.

The Babylonian gods/idols, Bel and Nebo, are powerless and have been unable to protect the Babylonians. They are being removed and carted off to captivity with the Babylonians themselves.

Isaiah is contrasting those man-made idols with the idols that the Israelites carry around. And like the Babylonian idols, our spiritual and emotional Idols are impotent, along with being heavy and burdensome to haul around.

Then in the next verses, God says through Isaiah that he is far from being like those idols:

Listen to me, O house of Jacob,
    all the remnant of the house of Israel,
who have been borne by me from before your birth,

> carried from the womb;
> even to your old age I am he,
> and to gray hairs I will carry you.
> I have made, and I will bear;
> I will carry and will save. (46:3–4)

God wants to support and carry us. God contrasts the man-made idols that must be carried with himself—the One who carries others. He is powerful, wise, and capable. Only he is alive and real, thus able to come through for us. All of our Idols and the Vows that created them are helpless, meaningless, and fragile. They cannot protect or provide for us.

When we make a Vow, we are reasoning, "Something bad happened to me, and I don't like what it says about me. Since God allowed that to happen, it's obvious that he isn't trustworthy. And since he's not meeting my needs, he must not be sufficient either. But something must be able to protect me and meet my need. I'm going to find what it is."

Is it always obvious when we are doing this? No, because it just seems like life. But we must identify these Idols. It could be People-Pleasing, our reputation, our image, control, having respect, being well-thought-of, a successful career, our children's success, our happiness—anything we value above God. We may not think it is an Idol, but it is if, when it is threatened, we feel tense and respond in unholy and unloving ways—if it provokes in us any reaction that is the opposite of the fruit of the Spirit. This reaction lets us know we worship it.

Many years ago I (Larry) counseled a man who pressured his wife to go into huge debt for a car that was beyond their means. He was so adamant that they purchase the car that, when she resisted, he told her, "I'm going to fast and pray this coming weekend, and if you don't agree to purchasing the car, I'm going to buy it regardless. And I don't even care if you divorce me over it."

He made good on his threat. After his weekend of fasting and praying, she refused to support his decision. He bought the car anyway and put his family deep into debt. Eventually, they did divorce, because of this and many other problems in their relationship.

When I heard this man's story, I was speechless. Then, as he shared his childhood, he talked about his father's love of cars and how he received the Message that a man's car is a reflection of a man's worth and value. As a result, he Vowed to always have a status-giving brand of car. He seemed totally clueless as to the seriousness of his Idol—his car. In his thinking it was completely reasonable to disregard his wife's opinion and to be unwilling to consider what God might be doing through his wife.

It would be easy for us to think right now, "Well, that man's response was ridiculous. I'm so glad I don't have any Idols like that." In fact, you may even be having a hard time thinking that you have any Idols at all.

Kathy's Input on This

I remember a day long ago when I was talking with a woman who was thought of as a kind of "irregular" person. We were in a group of Christians that day, and I felt good about myself that I was reaching out to a needy person. I was sacrificing to the Idol of my image when one of the men in the group came up to us. He took over the conversation. I don't remember exactly how, but in effect he dismissed me to leave.

Later in the evening, this fellow came up to me and said, "I knew you'd want to get away from her."

Only being in a group right at that moment (after all, I had to keep up appearances) prevented me from yelling at him. But in a heated voice, I retorted, "I didn't need your rescue. I was doing just fine."

He stared at me in surprise and then excused himself and turned away.

My reaction felt totally reasonable at the time, but I would not have been able to tell you why I was so bothered by what he had done. Only after I came to understand my motives better did I know why his "rescue" made me so angry. He had robbed me of an opportunity to sacrifice to my Idol of looking like a loving person. Through rescuing me, he was sending the message, I believed, that I didn't really want to be talking to that poor woman, thus removing the visible value of my sacrifice. I was mad because he had blocked my ability to be seen as magnanimous and compassionate. Since God has been diminishing this Idol in my life, I believe I would react differently in that situation today.

Do you get upset when your opportunity to be seen a certain way is spoiled? Or maybe you withdraw from a relationship because your "preferred image" is not being acknowledged?

These are hard questions. But they go to the core of how even we Christians can have Idols in our lives.

The Questions

Do you remember the questions we asked you to answer in Chapter One? Which do you think could help reveal your Vows? Actually many of those questions could do this, but let's look at a few.

What does it seem like or feel like you should have? "Should have" could point you to what you Demand. You may have written words like love, lack of conflict, or respect. Whatever your word(s), try to identify the Demands you put upon others or yourself. In your mind, how must you be perceived?

What do you hate? That which we hate might be that which we have Vowed to have for ourselves or how we have Vowed we will never be seen. What we hate we try to avoid in others or ourselves. Some people have answered this question with words like hypocrites, fakeness, insincerity, evil, pain, lies, or maybe the name of a person. Most of the time, what we hate is what we are convinced we don't exhibit ourselves; or the person we hate is someone we believe we aren't like. Yet, that assumption makes us blind to our own Vows, faults, and struggles. And we could resist any effort by the Holy Spirit to bring us to holiness in that area.

What have you promised yourself? That which you have promised yourself could very well be that which you have Vowed.

> "I've promised myself I'll never parent the way my
>   mom parented me."
> "I've promised myself I'll never drink alcohol because
>   my dad was a drunk."
> "I've promised myself I'll always make Christ my
>   highest priority because I don't want to be seen as
>   a hypocrite."

Such answers could reveal how we have determined what we will be like and, like the apostle Peter, we are convinced God would not want anything else. But such answers often demand perfection and reveal that we are operating on our own power.

How do you hate being seen by others? Again, answers for this question could reveal a Vow. Some possible answers are: not good enough, imperfect, incompetent, a flake, or arrogant. We are not looking to God to define us; we are making sure we define ourselves in an acceptable way to others. That is a part of People-Pleasing, and it leaves out God's view of us as "in Christ."

Do your answers take on a different light now that you see them as possible Vows? And how do you see becoming Hooked connected with those Vows?

God is creative in helping us to identify our Vows. Recently Kathy's blogger friend Cathy Horning wrote about a Vow (but she didn't know it).

For as far back as I can remember, I have always wanted others to see me as strong. Last summer God decided it was time to expose a chink in my "strong" exterior armor. Through a chain of events, God revealed that in my attempt to appear strong, I had managed to suppress much of the pain in my life. God forced me to see that over my lifetime I had mastered the ability to bury, deep down inside, any inconvenient, uncomfortable and irresolvable pain.

Subconsciously, I had designed a system to swiftly sweep away any unwelcome pain under an imaginary carpet in my heart. Until that summer day, when I carefully went to whisk fresh pain underneath my "carpet." Abruptly, I discovered there was no more room. To my dismay, years and years of carefully hidden hurt, disappointment, and grief came spilling out. And I found myself engulfed in heartbreaking anguish that could no longer be contained. And for hours, a torrent of tears and deep sobs shook my body.

That was the beginning of sudden, unpredictable, and hard-to-control outbursts of tears and a deep ache over the next days, weeks, and months. Helpless to stop it, I slowly realized I had no more capacity to keep my pain neatly hidden. Decades of loss, sorrow, and grief which I had never allowed myself to feel, look at, or deal with continued to surface, threatening to undo me, demanding to be attended to.

When I read Cathy's blog, I commented to her, "I have similar Vows of being capable and dependable—which is all about me and not depending upon God."

Cathy replied: "Kathy, I never thought about my desire to appear strong as a Vow. Wow, that sheds a new light on what I am learning. Thank you for reminding me that part of this process is depending on God, not on myself."

Cathy had not understood that her decision to be seen as strong established a Vow. But now that she has seen it, God is revealing the power of that Vow and helping her to renounce it.

Reflections and Group Discussion Questions

1. How would you have defined a "vow" before reading this chapter? Did you think the concept was very important in the Christian life?

2. What do you think the wording of your Vow is like most of the time? "I will . . ."? "I never . . ."? "I must . . ."? Or something else?

3. Look at the example of Vow beginnings at the start of this chapter. Can you complete any?

4. What is your reaction when you realize you have formed Vows? Explain your answer.

5. Can you give an example of how one of your Vows recently caused you to become Hooked?

6. Having which of your Vows unfulfilled feels the most dangerous to you?

7. Pick one of your Vows that you have identified and explain how it leaves out God.

8. Explain how one of your Vows creates a demand on other people.

9. What is one of your Entitlements? How does it affect your life and leave out God?

10. What would you like to say to God in prayer about what you have learned in this chapter? Write it down here.

Chapter 6

The Strategy—Part 1

We are not necessarily doubting that God will do the best for us; we are wondering how painful the best will turn out to be.

—C. S. Lewis

Sin is rebellion against God's will, the manifestation of humanity's revolt against its Creator. It has been said that sin is not just breaking the rules, it is making one's own rules.

—Anthony Carter

In her book *Blue Like Play Dough,* Tricia Goyer writes of a traumatic childhood experience that birthed a lifelong Strategy. Tricia's mother asked her new husband to drive Tricia to a friend's birthday party. Following the mother's vague description, he indicated he knew where to go and started driving as Tricia sat with the wrapped gift in her lap. He dropped her off at what seemed to resemble the description given by her mother, and Tricia walked to the front door of the house as her stepfather drove away.

The woman who answered the door was no one Tricia knew. She told the little girl she must be at the wrong house. The kind woman offered to drive Tricia somewhere else, but Tricia turned and hurried away.

Tricia writes, "I still held the present, but I didn't care about it anymore. I just wanted to be in a safe place.

"My chin trembled, but I set it determinedly. A car pulled up beside me. It was the woman from the house. She called out, 'Where are you going? Get in. I'll give you a ride.'

"I knew better than to get in and just ignored her."

Somehow Tricia's wandering led her to an area she knew—where her aunt lived. She rushed into her aunt's house, surprising her aunt. After a while Tricia's mother arrived and took her to the party that had already begun.

"All eyes turned and stared as I entered. I wanted to run and hide. They urged me to come and join their game. I refused.

"I sat in a little chair and watched the others from a distance. I'd found my way to safety this time, but what if another time I was too far away? I knew I never wanted anything like that to happen to me again. Others couldn't be trusted. I would take care of myself. I could trust myself.

"I was only five, but I took the lesson to heart."

Tricia's Strategy of trusting in herself took the form of getting herself off to school, taking care of her brother, and as she describes it, "making my own plans, finding my own way, depending on my own resources. So it was only natural that as a teenager I tried to fill my needs for love and attention by turning to guys."

Tricia learned a Strategy at an early age for protecting herself: trust only herself. Unfortunately, all of us have Strategies we learned from our own traumatic childhood experiences. And remember, even good experiences can encourage us to devise a scheme which leaves out trust in God. Fortunately, Tricia Goyer has committed to learning to trust Christ to diminish her Strategy of trusting only herself. Both in that book and in her other books, she shares her journey.

As we are identifying our own Strategies, it helps to think of the synonyms for the concept of a "Strategy": "methods, plans, schemes, systems, tactics, maneuverings" (from thesaurus. com). All of us choose various ways to cope with life and find ways to meet our own needs. All of us devise Strategies. Yes, there are biblical "strategies" like "taking every thought captive to obey Christ" (2 Cor. 10:5), and these are built upon and dependent on trusting God. But our "natural" strategies are sinful because we are not depending on God.

Remember our model?

The Wound creates a Message (giving birth to Wrong Beliefs and Distorted Images), resulting in a Vow, creating a Sinful Strategy, causing us to become Hooked.

Are we always going to make all these connections as we examine our lifelong journeys to greater holiness? No. A lot of the time we will just need to confess to God our sinful reaction, receive his cleansing, and then obey, even if we don't know the underlying cause of our difficulties. But distinguishing the underlying causes, we believe, often diminishes the strength of the Strategy so that we can more quickly obey.

As we talk about different kinds of Strategies, many of them may not be surprising to you. They will just seem like plain sin. And they are. You're exactly right. And yes, we must see them as sin. But a Stategy is not just a sin that we commit once. It's a pattern of behavior that we go back to again and again. That is why we call it a Strategy. If we don't see the Strategy's pervasive hold upon us, we will just grit our teeth and commit to "never doing" it again or "always doing" the opposite instead of pulling out the root of the problem.

Isaiah 36:4–6 gives us the result of depending on a Strategy. Those verses describe it as a broken staff or reed. If we lean on that kind of staff, it will break and pierce our hand, heart, and mind. It only brings pain.

> And the Rabshakeh said to them, "Say to Hezekiah, 'Thus says the great king, the king of Assyria: On what do you rest this trust of yours? Do you think that mere words are strategy and power for war? In whom do you now trust, that you have rebelled against me? Behold, you are trusting in Egypt, that broken reed of a staff, which will pierce the hand of any man who leans on it. Such is Pharaoh king of Egypt to all who trust in him.'"

What is ironic about those three verses is that one enemy of the Israelites (the Assyrians) is telling the Israelites that they are being foolish for depending upon someone else (the Egyptians). It's like the pot calling the kettle black. Both the Assyrians and the Egyptians are like Sinful Strategies to the Israelites. Both of them will let the Israelites down—like trying to lean on a broken staff or reed.

It's All about the Heart

A person's motivation determines whether a reaction is a Strategy. Sometimes a reaction can appear good but, because of the motives of that person's heart, it is actually a Sinful Strategy. This is an important distinction because many people defend their Strategies and the Strategies of others because they seem acceptable, positive, and even godly.

But God knows the heart, and he longs for pure fellowship with us. Hear his plea and his description of himself.

> "Yet even now," declares the LORD,
> "return to me with all your heart,
> with fasting, with weeping, and with mourning;
> and rend your hearts and not your garments."
> Return to the LORD your God,
> for he is gracious and merciful,
> slow to anger, and abounding in steadfast love;
> and he relents over disaster. (Joel 2:12–13)

That is why it is so important for us to examine our hearts, especially since Strategies are so subtly deceptive. For instance, it is hard to think that being dependable could be a Strategy. But, as I have told you already, ever since I was a girl I have loved being seen as dependable. When I lied in third grade, my Vow became, "I will never be seen as a liar, so I will be dependable. I'll protect my image in that way." Did I say those actual words? No, but that was the motive of my heart. As a Christian, for a long time I would sacrifice obeying God if it meant appearing undependable to others. I valued other people's opinions more than obeying God.

I (Larry) had my own Strategy of being seen as knowledge-able. On the surface this would seem like a good idea. But my inner commitment to possess a comprehensive knowledge of politics and economics was the seedbed for my Sinful Strategy. For then I could be persuasive; and being persuasive meant I was powerful. It was primarily a demand that no one see me as weak—like the weak man the coach almost drowned that day. But such a goal disregarded my inheritance in Christ and therefore was manipulative and rotten to the core.

Here are some other examples of mixed motives. A friend of ours turns generosity into a Strategy because he does it to earn applause from others. Another friend loves to give compliments (which seems positive), but she turns it into a Strategy because in her heart of hearts she wants to hear a compliment about herself. Still another friend pushes away compliments to appear humble.

Only God knows a person's heart. "The heart is deceitful above all things, and desperately sick; who can understand it?" (Jer. 17:9). This is why we can't judge another person's behavior. We don't know their heart condition and motive. And we must seek the Spirit's enlightenment to recognize our own motives.

To get to the core of what motivates us, we must recognize the way each Strategy diminishes—even destroys—our dependence upon God. Then we can get to the root of our own sinful plans and turn to God. Paul warns the Corinthian believers not to "be outwitted by Satan," not to be "ignorant of his designs" (2 Cor. 2:11). The New American Standard Bible uses the word "schemes" where the English Standard Version has "designs." We must heed the apostle Paul's warning in order to strengthen our hearts to recognize the ways we are deceived by Satan's schemes.

You Won't Be Surprised . . .

You won't be surprised to hear that Sinful Strategies are connected with Satan. In the midst of a passage describing the armor of God, Ephesians 6:11 tells us why. "Put on the whole armor of God, that you may be able to stand against the schemes of the devil," Paul instructs us. That word "schemes," also described as "wiles" in the King James Version, is the Greek word *methodia,* and we can easily see how it also describes our own personal Strategies, encouraged by Satan himself.

Vine's Expository Dictionary of New Testament Words tells us that this word "scheme" denotes "craft, deceit." The root words are "meta," meaning *after,* and "hodos," meaning a *way.* We could say that this *methodia*—this scheme—is a method of going after a way to handle something. And each of us is good at it—from childhood.

It is interesting that the word "scheme" is never used to describe God's plans. Although God has good plans, Satan's are always deceptive; after all, he is the "father of lies" (John 8:44). The only other time *methodia* is used in the Bible is in Ephesians 4:14: "So that we may no longer be children, tossed to and fro by the waves and carried about by every wind of doctrine, by human cunning, by craftiness in deceitful schemes."

For ease of discussion, we will categorize these Strategies into three motivations:

- Prevent
- Provide
- Promote

In this chapter, we will address the "Prevent" category. In the next chapter, we will talk about the "Provide" and "Promote" collection. Remember that Strategies can bleed over into one or more of the three categories. They aren't always clear-cut, but by examining them in light of those categories, we can better identify them.

Though the Strategies we examine may seem clearly evident as you read about them, right when we are being controlled by them, we often can't recognize them. Or we will see them but not admit they are sinful, because we can't get in touch with our motives. This is another part of the heart's deception. As one of our counselees said, "I didn't even realize I was omitting God from my everyday life. I just thought I was supposed to figure it out by myself."

When you see one of the Strategies named, don't judge too quickly or easily whether it applies to you. We think you will be surprised at how we slip into them without being aware that we have done so. Read about each one carefully, while prayerfully asking, "God, do you see me doing this? Is this a way I am leaving you out?"

Let's look together at some Strategies in the "Prevent" category.

Anger

One of the main Self-Protective Strategies is anger. We often call this the puffer fish syndrome. The puffer fish blows itself up to scare away another fish that could eat it. It's intended to instill fear and prevent danger. For me (Kathy) this is my default Strategy. For me (Larry) my default Strategy is in the Promote category which we'll cover in the next chapter.

Most anger is motivated by two basic purposes:

Blocked goal. We want something (our Idol) that seems necessary for our well-being. When something/someone blocks our getting it, we feel threatened and react with anger. We believe the anger communicates how important our goal is and will convince the other person to cooperate. We feel powerful rather than powerless.

Fear of being exposed. We Vowed to never be seen in a certain way, so we react in anger to divert attention from ourselves.

Our motivation is: "Don't see me as worthless, weak, insignificant, unlovable, imperfect," or a whole host of other things. When you get Hooked, stop and ask yourself, "How do I not want to be regarded right now?"

Let's look at those two elements in the biblical story of Balaam. But we will do it by working backward in the story. Toward the end of the story Balaam responds in an ungodly way, striking his donkey three times with a staff. We'll look at this first. Then we will replay the elements of the story that set up Balaam's Sinful Strategy of anger.

> Then the LORD opened the mouth of the donkey, and she said to Balaam, "What have I done to you, that you have struck me these three times?" And Balaam said to the donkey, *"Because you have made a fool of me. I wish I had a sword in my hand, for then I would kill you."* And the donkey said to Balaam, "Am I not your donkey, on which you have ridden all your life long to this day? Is it my habit to treat you this way?" And he said, "No." (Num. 22:28–30, emphasis added)

Balaam feels like he is being exposed as a fool. For "made a fool of," many versions use the wording "being mocked," thus giving the idea the prophet thinks the donkey is pouring contempt and disrespect upon him. The Amplified Bible words it: "Because you have ridiculed and provoked me!"

Secondly, Balaam's goal of reaching Balak so that he can be honored is being hindered. It could be a goal that he worships and is an Idol for him.

Now let's look back to see why we can arrive at these conjectures.

- *Balak's invitation appeals to Balaam's pride.* The king tells him, "I know that he whom you bless is blessed, and he whom you curse is cursed" (22:6). Balak is saying, "I recognize you as someone who has power."
- *Balak sends more leaders after Balaam at first replies no.* "Once again Balak sent princes, more in number and more honorable than these" (22:15). He is saying, "Hey, Balaam. Don't you realize how *really* important you are?"
- *Balak offers honors and riches.* The messengers say, "Let nothing hinder you from coming to me, for I will surely do you great honor, and whatever you say to me I will do" (22:16–17). Many versions indicate that "honor" includes "riches."

Balak wanted Balaam to come and curse the Israelites. He offered Balaam something Balaam evidently wanted: approval, distinction, and prosperity. Did Balaam already know what God's directive was? Yes. The Israelites were God's people, and they were blessed by God. God had told Balaam he should not curse his people. Nothing was going to change that. But Balaam succumbed to temptation. He agreed to seek the Lord again and, even though it seems incongruent that God told him to go (but not curse the Israelites), we know that God is always faithful.

Balaam is on the road to work with King Balak when the donkey sees an angel of the Lord with a drawn sword blocking their way. The donkey's actions save Balaam's life, yet without spiritual eyes to see the angel, Balaam only thinks his goals of attaining what he craves and worships will be blocked. And he hates being made a fool of by his donkey that should only obey him, thus giving him honor. Interestingly, he can get King Balak to give him honor, but he can't get a silly donkey to do the same!

Earlier in the text a little-noticed fact is included—one we might not consider important until now: "He was riding on the donkey, and his two servants were with him" (verse 22).

Balaam is not alone. Not only is the angel of the Lord there—whom Balaam can't see, Balaam's servants are there—whom Balaam can *definitely* see. Balaam's unexpressed Vow to not be seen as a fool, or as a person deserving to be mocked or ridiculed, is being exposed. After all, aren't these treatments the opposite of being approved, distinguished, and prosperous?

So Balaam strikes the donkey at least partly because he feels shamed and ridiculed in front of his servants. He blames a helpless donkey for his anger: "Stupid donkey! You provoked me! If only you hadn't disobeyed me, I wouldn't have to hit you. My anger is justified. It's all your fault!" It would seem that he is blatantly making sure his servants understand that it's not him, Balaam, who is stupid. It's this donkey! His actions actually communicate to his servants: "Don't look at me. I'm not stupid or worthless. You want to see stupid and worthless? Just look at the beast I'm riding."

Little by little, Balaam's underlying motives were unearthed. His itches for importance, pride, and comfort are being scratched. They are his Idols, and he does not really desire to please God.

We are good at hitting the messengers of God's will or getting angry at the circumstances that are blocking the fulfillment of what we crave—even though God is sovereignly designing the situation. Not really believing that God is in charge or that he knows what is best, we strike out in anger because it threatens us just to think that our needs won't be met.

I (Kathy) am like Balaam. I want to be seen as perfect, dependable, and knowledgeable. What makes me angry? I get mad when my actions reveal that I am imperfect, undependable, and stupid. If I don't surrender and allow God to expose me, I lash out to protect myself and try to provide for my own needs through anger.

How do you want to be seen? What makes you angry or frustrated when your goals are blocked or you are exposed in a way that embarrasses you or makes you appear to be a fool? It happens to every single one of us, because God wants us to look to him for what defines us and for what is best for us. He uses our circumstances to mold us into the image of Jesus—even while we are being ridiculed.

Here's a question for us. What are we angry about that actually might be God's protection and deliverance? Here are some possibilities:

- The person driving in front of me who slows down and causes me to miss the green light. (But being delayed might keep me from getting into a car accident.)
- Someone criticizes me. (But then I become aware of a fault I have been blind to.)
- An email that seems essential doesn't go through. (But then I learned some new information, so I realize now that the email would have been hurtful.)

What can you think of? At the time we may have felt that anger was appropriate because we had been wronged, delayed, misunderstood, mistreated (you name it). But anger is never godly when it is not quickly dealt with (Eph. 4:26). And contrary to Balaam's belief, no one causes us to get angry—not even a disobedient donkey. Anger is a choice based on our trying to provide for our own needs or trying to prevent negative exposure.

Taking Offense

On the Sunday morning of the couples' retreat where we were sharing the principles from this book, Daniel and his wife, Rebecca, pulled us aside. He began pouring out his heart, even as he frequently looked around to make sure no one was within earshot. Rebecca wrung her hands and stood beside Daniel while he explained, "I am so offended by a particular man at this church, Larry. He's even here at the retreat, so I'm planning for us to leave after I talk with you. This fellow has hurt my feelings by first befriending us and then telling lies about us."

We didn't have much time before the next session started so, though risking a lot, I put my hand on Daniel's shoulder, trying to soften the brunt of my words. Looking him in the eyes, I asked him, "Why do you allow someone else to control your life?"

Daniel stared back at me as he processed my words. "Oh," he mused. "I guess I do, don't I? I've never thought of it that way before."

"Do you know why?" I asked him.

"Well, you've talked this weekend about Strategies, and I guess that is one of mine. When people don't treat me the way I think they should, I get upset and run away. I don't want them to see me as the wimp I've always felt inside. That's the Vow you two talked about, right? I did get that. In fact, your sharing helped me see that I vowed I would never be like my wimpy father."

"So where does your Strategy come in?" Kathy interjected.

Daniel was obviously calmer now and scratched his head in thought. "Okay, let's see," he reflected. "The opposite of being a wimp is being powerful, and being angry and offended makes me feel powerful. I guess I think that's showing strength, but actually it's not. I see that now. And besides, it backfires on me—like if we were to leave here now and miss the rest of the conference."

I continued, "Just one more question, Daniel. How does your being offended leave out God?"

"Oh." He rubbed his eyes and blinked. "Well, I guess I'm not seeking what God wants me to do in the situation. And I'm not seeing myself the way God sees me. I get it."

Daniel and Rebecca stayed for the rest of the retreat and later told us they benefited from it.

Being offended is actually a defensive way of saying, "You're seeing me in a way that I am determined you won't see me." Or, "You're treating me in a way that I am determined no one will treat me." It's a form of anger that uses an ungodly method (remember *methodia*?) to prevent being exposed or having a goal blocked.

Pastor and author Tim Keller writes in *The Freedom of Self-Forgetfulness*:

> People sometimes say their feelings are hurt. But our feelings can't be hurt! It is the ego that hurts—my sense of self, my identity. . . . It is very hard to get through a whole day without feeling snubbed or ignored or feeling stupid or getting down on ourselves. That is because there is something wrong with my ego. There is something wrong with my identity.

Instead of the words "being offended," we can use other words that seem acceptable, even righteous, such as "being hurt." Regardless of the wording, getting our egos bruised easily turns into resentment and bitterness if it is not curtailed by accepting God's view of us and trusting his sovereign control over everything that happens to us.

Along with not abiding in our inheritance in Christ, being offended is also a way of saying, "God doesn't know what he's doing because I am too important and valuable to be treated like this." It's a diversionary tactic that says, "Don't see me the way this situation seems to be reflecting me."

Isaiah 49:7 says:

> Thus says the LORD,
>> the Redeemer of Israel and his Holy One,
> to one deeply despised, abhorred by the nation,
>> the servant of rulers:
> "Kings shall see and arise;
>> princes, and they shall prostrate themselves;
> because of the LORD, who is faithful,
>> the Holy One of Israel, who has chosen you."

God is identifying how Israel thinks of itself: despised, abhorred, and a servant. After all, at this time, it is true. The Israelites *are* despised, abhorred, and in servitude, because they are exiles in Babylon. Without trust and faith in God, they could be justified in describing themselves with those terms.

But what is God's solution and perspective in that verse? The ones who regard Israel as abhorred will eventually "prostrate" themselves by honoring Israel. Why? Because God has their back. He has chosen Israel as his own. It's all about God's view of Israel, not about anything else.

Later in the chapter, Zion/Israel whines, "But Zion said, 'The LORD has forsaken me; my Lord has forgotten me'" (49:14).

Zion complains that because of the difficult circumstances she is going through, God has abandoned her. Her moaning sounds like she is looking for justification for being hurt and offended.

What is God's reply?

> Can a woman forget her nursing child,
>> that she should have no compassion on the son of
>> her womb?
> Even these may forget,
>> yet I will not forget you.
> Behold, I have engraved you on the palms of
> my hands;
>> your walls are continually before me.
> Your builders make haste;
>> your destroyers and those who laid you waste go
>> out from you.
> Lift up your eyes around and see;
>> they all gather, they come to you.
> As I live, declares the Lord,
>> you shall put them all on as an ornament;
>> you shall bind them on as a bride does. (49:15–18)

At this point in Israel's history, the Jews *are* exiled captives in Babylon and the walls of Jerusalem *are* crumbled and ruined. From all outward appearances, their self-evaluation is correct. Just like the areas of our lives when we are needy, destroyed, or hopeless—and everyone else knows it, to our chagrin.

But God says his view of them is more important than theirs and that he has a purpose for the difficult circumstances they are facing.

Here are his points:

- *You are on my mind as much as a mother nursing her child.* A mother thinks a lot about the needs of a nursing child.
- *You are engraved on the palms of my hands.* Have you noticed that your hands are continually out in front of your sight?
- *You don't see what I see.* He has a plan.
- *You will look as glorious as a gilded, ornamented bride.* Have you noticed that a happy bride is the most radiant person on earth? That's how the Israelites will become. They will radiate God's glory.

As you think of your own temptations to be hurt, offended, resentful, or bitter, can you identify the root source? More than likely you can point to a Wound, that birthed a Message, that created a Vow, and turned into a Strategy, in the form of anger. And it is all wrapped in the cloak of distrust of God's sovereign control and a denial of how he sees you. But don't despair. There is hope and power for overcoming this. Continue with us.

Unfortunately, we must consider one more anger response.

Contempt

Contempt shows up when we express a lack of respect for someone. In subtle or obvious ways we communicate that we think they are inferior or unworthy of value. You may think you don't act with contempt, but consider:

- Do you ever roll your eyes?
- Do you have unrealistic expectations?
- Do you gossip?
- Do you belittle the efforts of another person?

- Do you make fun of the idiosyncrasies of others?
- Do you interrupt others?
- Do you use disrespectful words when you are talking about others?

If you have done any of those, you have acted with contempt. Contempt is another extremely subtle form of anger. It is the most devious form of diversion, because it can be wrapped so easily in the cloak of self-righteousness.

Author and psychologist Dr. Dan Allender writes in *The Wounded Heart*, "Contempt is absurd in that it inevitably increases man's vulnerability while it enables him to regain a semblance of control that protects him against dependence on God. Contempt is a major weapon against the humbling work of God."

Ross is a man who uses contempt artfully. He is a cold man with a veneer of friendliness. When we met him, we had no idea what a deep pool of contempt lay below that veneer. As we began counseling him, however, it came ever so slowly to light. His whole response to life is contemptuous. Ross's boss doesn't know anything. If Ross were boss, everything would be right at work. Why are Ross's work results weak? Well, that's because his coworkers don't do what they are supposed to do, so it isn't his fault.

He tries to cover up his contempt by using humor: "Oh, my boss is such a dingbat; he doesn't know his right hand from his left foot." "Oh, my coworker is one step away from disaster. It follows her around like a hungry puppy ready for its next meal." You could easily begin to believe that he is surrounded by every knucklehead in the universe and he is the only one who knows what he's doing.

The truth is that Ross has not earned a paycheck for a year because he is on commission. When asked why he doesn't get another job, he declares, "I will never quit! As soon as my boss gets the office in shape, I'll make plenty of money, and then I'm going to be a missionary in Africa. That's what I really want to do—to bring glory to God."

As we explored his Vow of "never quitting," we unearthed a deep Wound from his father. Ross had wanted to stop attending chess club because the math teacher had changed the club meetings to a time that interfered with Ross' football practice. When Ross tried to explain that he had to be quitting *something*, his father sneered at him since he had forced Ross to join the chess club. He told Ross, "You will be a total failure for the rest of your life if you ever quit. The only way to succeed is to stay focused and determined."

Ross felt a deep sense of voicelessness, because his words were inadequate to explain this catch-22. His Vow of never quitting was his feeble effort to show his father that he really was focused and determined.

Ross' frequent use of contempt is his Strategy to prevent being seen as a quitter and to divert attention from his blocked goal of success.

You may not think you are like Ross, and maybe you aren't. But pay attention to the words that reveal your heart. Do you see yourself as better than others? Do you think you know more than people around you? Do you often think that if someone would just do what you think they should, they would be healthy, happy, and holy?

Are you willing to have your own sins pointed out? Can you admit that you don't always have the right answer?

You can Repent and Surrender. We will soon be talking about that, and you will learn that honestly facing your Strategy of contempt will start the heart change.

Hypervigilance

Hypervigilance is a heightened awareness of a person's sur-roundings, especially with a sense of warding off danger or a threat. The Hypervigilant person most often thinks or uncon-sciously believes, "If I let down my guard, I will get hurt. Therefore, I must do everything I can to evaluate what's going on around me."

See if you can identify with or relate to these thoughts:

- Am I giving appropriate feedback?
- Does she/he like me?
- What is her/his intention?
- What's going on that he/she is not revealing to me?
- He/she doesn't really like me.
- Why is he/she acting like that?
- Am I safe to share my heart and my problems?
- What did he really mean by that?

Can you see how Hypervigilance says, "I will not let you, God, be in charge. It's too scary and it feels like death"?

That word "death" may seem too strong, but we have actu-ally had people tell us that when they are challenged by God to do the opposite of their Strategy, they feel threatened to the point of feeling it will bring death—death of some sort: emo-tional, physical, or mental. It is that threatening. This seems to be especially true for sexual-abuse victims. If they aren't aware and protecting themselves, they could face consequences that literally feel like death— at least, a death of their soul.

Pastor Mike Wilkerson writes in *Redemption*, "In deliver-ing you, God wants to show you that this manner of life, which may be all you've ever known, is actually death. He wants you to walk away. But walking away from the only life you've known can feel like death. This is all very risky. It may feel like it's getting worse before it gets better."

Those who do not choose this Strategy find it hard to believe that someone can be so adept at reading the intentions of other people—or at least *thinking* they are reading them accurately. Since I can succumb to this Strategy, I may mention to Larry, "Did you notice our friend's subtle reaction to her husband's comments about her weight? She was so unhappy." And Larry will reply, "Really? I didn't notice."

My Hypervigilance can take the form of wanting to step in to help or to be whatever another person needs, but without seeking God's guidance. Whenever I sense that a person is depressed, I may feel tense, thinking I need to do something to draw them out of their misery. Immediately, I feel responsible, rather than first making sure I'm the one God wants to respond. Over time, slowly, I have turned more from my desire to be their protector or provider. I have learned instead to remember that an opportunity is not necessarily God's open door. God may want them to seek only him for their situation, or maybe I'm just supposed to be praying for them. I am sinning if I think I am the answer to their prayers—and the only answer.

I am also sinning if my motivation is, "But what will they think about me if I ignore their pain?" Then it's not really about seeing God glorified, it is about protecting how I am seen.

The Physical Body

Listen to Shelby's words: "I do run from things. Maybe that's why I loved running as a teenager. My mom's major nervous breakdown kept her on our couch with the rooms darkened for five years. Then my parents tried to put their marriage back together after my dad cheated with a coworker. I would get home from high school, throw my books on my bed, put on shorts, and out the door I'd go. I would run around our neighborhood for at least an hour. Sometimes I'd be crying, trying to figure out a way to protect myself from all the darkness, pain, and betrayal at home. I didn't know when the next crisis would hit.

"It felt so good to run and think and run til I couldn't run any more—as if I could solve all the problems at home while I was jogging. Then I'd go home and take a nap, come out only to eat, go back in my room, and start my homework. Hiding was my comfort. That would take me until almost midnight, because I read so darn slow. But I wanted straight As. I had my driver's license and a little car, but I would choose to take the school bus instead because I loved the bus driver like an older sister. I enjoyed talking with her on the way to and from school.

"Why do I run? Why do I even run from meeting with friends who have asked me numerous times to meet them for lunch or coffee? I should never complain about not having a friend to do things with if I won't make time for them when they've asked. Most of the time I tell myself it's lack of money that prevents me. But actually, it's because I feel uncomfortable being seen as not having the money even to get coffee."

Shelby's Strategy is to run, both physically and emotionally. Other physical Strategies include anorexia, bulimia, obesity, pulling out eyelashes, cutting the skin, and a variety of ways people abuse their own bodies. Sexual-abuse victims often use anorexia, bulimia, or obesity/being overweight as a means of hiding the desirability of their bodies. If they cover it up, they won't be seen, they reason, so they will be protected from having their body used for evil. Self-abusive actions like pulling out eyelashes or cutting one's skin distract from emotional pain. When masochists are thinking about the pain in their flesh, they don't seem to be as aware of their emotional pain.

Even something as seemingly innocuous as pulling on an ear or rubbing the eyes can be a Strategy to give self-comfort or to distract from a disappointment without seeking God's comfort and presence. Of course, all those things might not be anything other than having a scratch that needs to be itched. It depends on the motive. It depends on the heart.

Listen to Amie Patrick's story. Though now a pastor's wife and mother of four, her college years were a struggle about weight. Within the first two months of her freshman year, Amie gained twenty pounds and began a twenty-year struggle to control her eating and weight. Little by little she recognized God's work, as she says, "from the inside out." It was no longer a matter of forcing herself to eat less but of seeing the underlying causes of her overeating—her Strategies.

She writes,

> I didn't struggle with food because I simply needed more information about healthy eating. I was an expert at counting calories, measuring portion sizes, and making healthy choices. And I didn't struggle with my weight because I was lazy or uninformed about exercise. At my heaviest weight, I was exercising rigorously on a daily basis. I overate to escape from the tremendous pressure I felt to perform and please in order to have the approval of others. I overate because I believed I needed the comfort of food in times of stress, sadness, or anxiety.
>
> Only when I was willing to look deeply at the root causes of my disordered eating and honestly confess

my sin and unbelief did anything start to change. Until then, I was stuck in the garden of my heart, pulling out the same weeds day after day and getting nowhere. Pulling weeds is important, but it's only one part of growing a beautiful garden. I didn't just need to change a few habits or drop a few pounds; my belief system needed to be uprooted and replanted with biblical truth. Responsible stewardship of our physical bodies is clearly biblical, but trying to achieve this goal by focusing solely on changing outward habits doesn't work for those living from a belief system that opposes the transforming truth of Scripture. The greatest need of a person caught in a trap is rescue, not a strategy for trap-management.

When Patrick says, "I didn't just need to change a few habits or drop a few pounds; my belief system needed to be uprooted and replanted with biblical truth," she is referring to the concept of Sin Management that we covered in Chapter Four. Thankfully, she didn't just manage her sin through losing weight, but she went deeply into the heart's motives by uprooting her beliefs and replanting a biblical belief system.

Obviously, more Protective Sinful Strategies exist than we could possibly cover here. In our next chapter, Part II on Strategies, we will identify Strategies in the Provide and Promote categories.

Reflections and Group Discussion Questions

1. What surprised you the most about this chapter?

2. Were you able to call something a "Strategy" that you hadn't identified before?

3. What did you learn about Balaam's story? Do you relate?

4. How do you express anger in your life? What motivates your anger?

5. Can you see in your life any Strategy of being hurt or offended? What is the heart attitude that contributes to that? Can you see the roots of a Wound, Message, or Vow in it?

6. Can you think of a time when you reacted with contempt?

7. Would you be willing to ask those closest to you whether you respond with contempt often?

8. To what degree are you Hypervigilant? In what situations do you fall into it most often? Again, what Wound, Message, or Vow do you see at the foundation of it?

9. Do you struggle with any physical Strategies? If so, what is at the source of them? Does identifying any Wound, Message, or Vow attached to the Strategy assist you in seeking God's healing?

Chapter 7

The Strategy—Part II

*Being a people-pleaser is like having a little
handle on your back that others can grab hold
of to push you and pull you in all directions.*

—Lou Priolo

*The greatest ethical challenge is so to live that men don't
glorify you for living that way, but God.*

—John Piper

As we continue our examination of Strategies, we are sure
it is no surprise to you that there are so many of them. After all,
most of them are just plain sin. Our fear of pain and the temptations of Satan provide plenty of fodder for learning creative
patterns that omit God from our lives. So let's look at the next
main category of the three (Protect, Provide, and Promote).

Provide
We have been amazed at the number of Scripture verses and
passages that describe Strategies. Here is another one:

Who among you fears the LORD
and obeys the voice of his servant?

129

Let him who walks in darkness
    and has no light
trust in the name of the LORD
    and rely on his God.
Behold, all you who kindle a fire,
    who equip yourselves with burning torches!
Walk by the light of your fire,
    and by the torches that you have kindled!
This you have from my hand:
    you shall lie down in torment. (Isa. 50:10–11)

Dan Allender writes in *The Wounded Heart* about those two verses:

> The so-called reasonable desire to avoid pain, discomfort, or shame compels us to light our own fire. Fire lighters are those who take charge of the dark (particularly, struggle or confusion in relationships) by their own means, for their own purposes. It seems that the natural desire to avoid pain directs us toward a path of independence, when, in fact, the desire for relief and satisfaction, if the hunger is deeply felt, will lead to a path of chosen dependence on a Person greater than ourselves.

Yes, that is what we desire—dependence on God—but it is a scary invitation. And sometimes even identifying the roadblocks is difficult because they are so subtle and so deeply ingrained. Plus, they seem so natural, because we have depended on them for so long. So let's continue to identify our Strategies, and in particular, those that are in the category of Provide. We will see how we prevent dependence on God by providing for ourselves.

Victimization

The Victim drinks from the cistern of a lack of action. For instance, our friend told us about her mother's attitude, which includes saying often, "One day my ship will come in." But she is eighty-one years old. The ship still has not arrived. Our friend explained, "She has always shirked responsibility because of the coming ship. Since her knight in shining armor will appear some day, there is no reason to do anything now. It prevents her from taking risks or attempting any kind of action."

Contributing to her mother's Strategy of Victimization is her dependence on comparing her troubles to the troubles of others. Her own troubles always appear to be more difficult, trying, exhausting, etc., and this feeds her belief that her own troubles are beyond help. Our friend explained that this is the Jewish strategy *tsuris*, a word for troubles or problems. It becomes a strategy of, "You think *you've* got troubles? *I've* got troubles!"

Seeing everything as full of *tsuris* provides an excuse . . .

- from having to deal with reality. "My problems are worse. It's the world's fault, not mine."
- from being intimate. "No reason to make friends; they can't understand my life."
- from accepting God's joy or believing he can provide. "My needs are beyond what anyone can provide for—even the Lord."
- from remembering past good things. "Even though something good has happened, it won't last."

The attitude of "this too will pass" is the opposite of *tsuris*. Instead of thinking everything is horrible and helpless, this philosophy focuses on gritting our teeth until the problem passes.

We don't need God. We provide our own fire by waiting long enough and toughing it out.

As I struggled to trust God for his provision of joy and contentment during those difficult days when I was a caregiver for Larry's mother, I thought, "This too will pass." And then on the heels of that thought came, "If I just knew how much longer Audrey is going to live, I could be more patient and kind." I was thinking I could be more patient because I would be gritting my teeth, just waiting for that trial to end. That's not depending upon God's provision, that's lighting my own fire.

I examined the phrase, "This too will pass," more deeply. Haven't we all said this and sighed in relief? Maybe we thought, "Okay, if I just hold on long enough, this trial/situation/challenge will come to an end." But that is not trusting God's provision; it's carrying our own torch.

No wonder God doesn't tell us the future. If we knew a trial was going to last a long time, we would give up. If we knew a trial was going to be short-lived, we would grin and bear it. We are supposed to relax in God's power moment by moment, depending on him, allowing him to provide the "fire" we need.

Self-Sufficiency

Of course, we do need to talk here about money, but self-sufficiency is more pervasive than just finances. It is a huge indicator of what we truly believe about God. Is he big enough and powerful enough to provide for us?

Remember the opening story in Chapter One where Kathy asked me why I would not pray for myself in dangerous situations? Most of my life I have struggled with carrying my own torch of self-sufficiency. Too often I will react and just start to handle a problem or event without considering how prayer might enter into the equation. I now see how forgetting to pray in dangerous situations demonstrated my lack of trust in God. My mouth proclaimed that I trusted God in my daily life, but my self-centered actions demonstrated that my heart believed God was not enough. I never had the conscious thought that God could not be trusted, but my reactions revealed my lack of trust. The wounding of that near-drowning and the school play failure caused me to trust myself to ensure that I would always be prepared and would not be exposed as less than a man. God was on my lips, but my commitment to protect myself revealed my heart's demand to walk in the light of my own torch.

Early in my ministry, I (Kathy) received a letter from a woman who had read one of my books. She talked about how she trusted God to provide for her and faithfully tithed, but she still had one crisis after another that kept her and her family struggling to pay their bills.

As I prayed for her, I wondered why God was not providing for this family. Then I had the opportunity of spending several hours with her. She told me, "I keep praying that the Lord will help me win the Publishers Clearing House Sweepstakes." She described to me how she spent multiple hours each day filling out forms and finding contests to enter. She bought lots of stamps.

I saw the truth. She was not really depending on God; she was treating him as a vending machine who should pay out because of her prayer deposits. She was lapping at the cistern of self-sufficiency through her Idol, those contests. I have no idea what her Wound was, and I did not know at that time how to call her to Repentance. I had questioned why God was not being faithful, but all along he was working in her life. If he had answered her prayer for provision through a contest, she would continue to look to that rather than to God.

Most likely the rich young ruler (Matt. 19:16–22) who came to Jesus had a Strategy of Self-Sufficiency. He was carrying his own torch, he was making his own fire, by following the Law and commandments. He expected Jesus to suggest that he follow those rules in order to gain eternal life. And Jesus at first did stay at the level of the Law by challenging him, "You shall not murder, you shall not commit adultery, you shall not steal, you shall not bear false witness, honor your father and mother, and you shall love your neighbor as yourself." Evidently the young man thought this was the easy answer on the quiz, because he claimed he had done those things.

He had no clue that Jesus was referring to this to do list as a barometer of the heart. This young man's behavior seemed obedient, but evidently he had not attended the class entitled "Sermon on the Mount" (Matt. 5–7). Jesus explains there that pleasing the Lord is all about the heart and not just the behavior. Jesus in his compassionate way was gently guiding this young man toward truth, although Jesus knew he would walk away.

The young man then asked, "What else do I lack?" You have to give him credit. He seemed determined, and he clearly knew there was something more. Jesus told him, "If you would be perfect, go, sell what you possess and give to the poor, and you will have treasure in heaven; and come, follow me" (Matt. 19:21).

This was a specific soul-care interaction designed exactly for this man because of his Idol, which had birthed a Strategy. We have no record that Jesus ever told anyone else to do this same thing. Why? Because other recorded interactions did not include a person who idolized and suffered from the Strategy of Self-Sufficiency.

Interestingly, Zacchaeus evidently did not suffer from this Strategy or, if he did, he quickly repented of it, because even though Jesus didn't tell him to "go, sell," Zacchaeus did it of his own accord (Luke 19:1–10). His heart was supernaturally healed and delivered—from the inside out. The fruit was generosity to others and commitment to Jesus.

The rich young ruler's heart was not changed. "When the young man heard this he went away sorrowful, for he had great possessions" (Matt. 19:22). His possessions were his god, and he did not want to surrender his Strategy of Self-Sufficiency. It must have felt to him like death to do that, and he ended up choosing eternal death, the opposite of the eternal life he sought from Jesus.

Promote

I was trying on some clothes when I overheard another woman in the next fitting room say to a child (who sounded about five years old), "Isn't this sexy? Won't I get everyone's attention?"

I was deeply grieved. What message had this woman just given this little girl? Value sexiness and be the center of attention.

After Kathy related that story to me, I thought of a conversation I had with one of the guys in my men's group. He has the most darling, vivacious five-year-old you would ever want to meet. She is just incredibly bubbly and, of course, gets lots of attention.

Is there anything wrong with a little girl's vivaciousness and her being the center of attention? No, of course not. But I encouraged this father to be careful to guide his daughter and to remind her that her value is not rooted in her performance, in being delightful or being seen, but in being a child of God.

Let's look now at Strategies in the category of Self-Promotion. People who employ this Strategy crave an identity that leaves out God by demanding that we are seen in a certain way. We may hunger for prominence, power, acclaim, perfection, praise, and a wide variety of other destructive goals. And, as in the case of every Strategy, we get Hooked and react in an ungodly manner when our chosen Idol of identity is threatened. Let's look at a few.

Appearing Loved

Heather Kopp, author of *Sober Mercies*, wrote on her blog:

> From my earliest days with Dave, I took Valentine's Day pretty seriously. I wanted it all—the romance, the flowers, the candy.
>
> When Dave failed his first important boyfriend test, I made sure he knew why this holiday mattered so much. "The whole world knows what day it is," I explained. "And women ask each other, 'What did he do? What did he get you?' If you do little or nothing, I feel embarrassed!"
>
> How twisted is that? I wanted tangible evidence of Dave's adoration mainly to prove to my friends that I was loved and lovable—Ack!
>
> Actually, it was worse than that. Dave quickly learned that even if he lavished me with gifts, a poem, or chocolate on Valentine's Day, he wasn't home free. He needed to behave in ways that made me feel romanced and pursued. If my heart failed to flutter, clearly he was only going through the motions . . . and he could expect a tantrum.
>
> In retrospect, I viewed Valentine's Day not as a day to celebrate love, but as an opportunity to test it. It was like I set a trap, and then lay in wait for

Dave to screw up—so I could pounce and feel hurt and offended.

What kind of wife or girlfriend acts like that?

At the time, my motives were a mystery even to me. But looking back, here's what I see. As an active alcoholic, I pretty much specialized in behaving badly. And since I knew that the "score" in our marriage was skewed in Dave's favor, I relished his mistakes. For at least a few hours, I got to feel a little less guilty.

Because the heart is wicked and deceived, Heather's ulterior motives for her Strategy of Appearing Loved were not easily identified. But God was faithful and delivered Heather from both her alcoholism and her cherished Strategy.

People-Pleasing

People-Pleasing is all about depending on the opinions of others for our approval, rather than on God. We fear making other people unhappy with us or causing them to think poorly of us. So we strive to do everything we can to appease other people and promote ourselves as important, valuable, or whatever Vow we've made to protect ourselves.

In the Bible we find many examples of People-Pleasing. The best-known one may be the time when King Saul succumbed to this Strategy. His reaction is featured in 1 Samuel 13:8–14:

He [Saul] waited seven days, the time appointed by Samuel. But Samuel did not come to Gilgal, and the people were scattering from him. So Saul said, "Bring the burnt offering here to me, and the peace offerings." And he offered the burnt offering. As soon as he had finished offering the burnt offering, behold,

Samuel came. And Saul went out to meet him and greet him. Samuel said, "What have you done?" And Saul said, "When I saw that the people were scattering from me, and that you did not come within the days appointed, and that the Philistines had mustered at Michmash, I said, 'Now the Philistines will come down against me at Gilgal, and I have not sought the favor of the LORD.' So I forced myself, and offered the burnt offering." And Samuel said to Saul, "You have done foolishly. You have not kept the command of the LORD your God, with which he commanded you. For then the LORD would have established your kingdom over Israel forever. But now your kingdom shall not continue. The LORD has sought out a man after his own heart, and the LORD has commanded him to be prince over his people, because you have not kept what the LORD commanded you."

Saul sinned when he disobeyed God's command that no one except God's designated ones could offer a sacrifice. What was Saul's reaction to being caught in sin? He defended himself, saying,

- *There was a justification*: the people were scattering. He didn't depend upon the Lord, and it must have seemed like the people were rejecting him personally—maybe revealing their lack of confidence in him.
- *Samuel didn't show up on time*. Actually he did but it was at the final hour.

- *"I have not sought the favor of the LORD."* He must have thought that making it a spiritual matter would make him appear godly and innocent.
- *"I forced myself."* As if he didn't really want to do it, thus indicating his motivation was right, when it wasn't.

What was God looking for? A man after God's own heart; but Saul's heart was all about himself and the approval of others. Interestingly, at one point, Saul received an attitude adjustment—a new heart—from the Lord (1 Sam. 10:9). As with all of us, even though we have become new creatures in Christ, we continue as a mixed bag of motives and reactions. Saul made a few wise decisions, and he certainly got credit for those. But in the most serious thing—offering a corrupted sacrifice—his heart was not fully God's. And God replaced him with David, "a man after God's own heart."

Where does the courage to choose God and not depend upon people's opinions start?

Lay hold of God's promise, "What can man do to me?" (Heb. 13:6). God is the only one who will love us perfectly. Only he can provide unconditional love and approval because we wear the "robe of righteousness" purchased for us by Jesus' redemptive death.

Have a heart after God by identifying the source of our reactions. We can be strengthened to obey and have God's perspective only by identifying and healing the Wounds that befall us.

At a couples' retreat we met a man whom we will call Michael. Everyone described him as a man with the gift of evangelism. As the weekend progressed, we could see why he was given that description. He had no fear at all about sharing the gospel. And he loved telling us multiple stories of the receptivity of the people he spoke to. As we got to know him better, he shared some stories from his childhood.

Michael grew up in an emotionally bankrupt family—a description that included his extended family. He told us that he rarely was praised, appreciated, or encouraged. Michael longed for acknowledgment of his accomplishments.

When he was six, his mother was seriously ill, to the point that everyone thought she would die. The family and extended family were in the hospital waiting room, expecting soon to say their goodbyes. Michael happened to be in her room when the doctor came and told his father, "Your wife will live." Evidently, she had been misdiagnosed and there was a cure. Overjoyed, Michael's father told Michael, "Go tell everyone your mother will live. They found a cure."

Michael ran to the waiting room and stood in the doorway. Everyone turned to him with glum faces, yet he burst out, "Mama will live. They found a cure!"

Everyone was thrilled, crowding around Michael, patting him on the head, hugging him, and some even picked him up in the air in jubilation. "Great news, boy, great news! Tell us more!"

As Michael shared this story with us while we were visiting him, his face was transfixed into joy and delight.

I asked him, "Wow, how fabulous. How did you feel?"

With the same beaming look on his face, Michael effused, "Larry, I felt like I'd given them the best news in the world. For years afterward, the family described me as the one who gave the good news about Mama's recovery."

Kathy and I looked at each other with a knowing glance. For him the opportunity to give the great report was like water on a parched piece of desert. The Message Michael received that day was that he was important. The Vow became, "I want to do everything I can to feel that way again." The Strategy after he came to know Christ was, "Tell everyone the good news of Jesus Christ, and they'll thank me for it." He wanted that feeling again and again because it provided needed satisfaction to his soul. Telling others about Jesus and also sharing with Christians how God had used him became Michael's Self-Promoting Strategy of approval and applause, and all of this came from a positive Wound. When telling other Christians about his evangelism adventures years later, Michael still was controlling how people saw him.

This story is another opportunity for us to emphasize the distinction of doing something positive from a wrong motivation. Obviously, not everyone who shares the gospel is doing it for the emotional-thirst-quencher of People-Pleasing. And we know that Michael sincerely wants people to go to heaven, but without hearing his story we would have no understanding of his mixed motivation. When we asked, "What would you do if God told you to not share the gospel at some point?"

He was horrified. "What? I couldn't do that. Sharing the gospel is just too important." His Idol was revealed. Sharing was more important than obeying God. Sharing was his way of going to the broken cistern and turning away from God's living spring.

The psalmist shows a "heart after God" kind of attitude in Psalm 69:10–13:

> When I wept and humbled my soul with fasting,
>   it became my reproach.
> When I made sackcloth my clothing,

> I became a byword to them.
> I am the talk of those who sit in the gate,
>   and the drunkards make songs about me.
> But as for me, my prayer is to you, O Lord.
>   At an acceptable time, O God,
>   in the abundance of your steadfast love answer me
>   in your saving faithfulness.

The psalmist looked to God for his approval and was not diverted by the disapproval of others. He obeyed God and fasted, even though it brought reproach. That is the challenge for any of us with a People-Pleasing Strategy.

Inadequacy

Most of the time we think a Self-Promoting Strategy is revealed through reactions of pride. But it can also be lived out in a Strategy of Inadequacy. Instead of thinking too highly of ourselves, we may hang out in the camp of putting ourselves down. And it is not humility. Not really.

I was invited by two friends who were great golfers to play with them in a golf tournament. Their invitation tensed me up and I explained to Kathy, "I feel unqualified to play; I'll pull them down in the competition."

I continued a litany of why I shouldn't play: "I'm the wrong guy," "They will be putting up with me." "I'm the weak link."

Kathy replied, "You're getting Hooked."

I was surprised. I tried to get in touch with that, but I didn't agree. "No, I don't think so. It's justified because I *really* could let the team down." Kathy obviously didn't understand the world of men. Competition was just too important.

She pursued it. "What Message would losing say about you?"

"Well, I would feel unworthy to be on the team. But y'see, I don't mind losing when it's only me playing. It's just that I'll drag down the team, and that is unacceptable. No, I don't think I'll play."

Kathy grinned as she put on her hat labeled "Counselor." "Okay, let's try a different tack. What reaction do you fear from your teammates if you play poorly?"

"No, honey, I just don't see that this is about their reaction at all. Sorry, no cigar."

Kathy let it drop with another smile. I could tell she was going to be praying for me!

But later that day as I continued to evaluate what was going on and to seek God's perspective, I saw how I actually was being Hooked because I didn't want to look inadequate. I didn't want them to think poorly of me and be displeased with me if I contributed to the team's loss.

When I told Kathy what I had discovered, she smiled her knowing smile and encouraged me to play on the team. I repented of my Idol of performance and People-Pleasing and surrendered to knowing that whatever God wanted to happen in the game would be good and used for his purposes.

As it turned out, I played pretty well but one of my teammates crashed. He couldn't make any good shots. I enjoyed the camaraderie and had a great day even though we didn't win any prize money.

Several familiar biblical examples speak to being seen well. Just like us, most of these Bible characters started out being willing to disobey God in order to prevent exposure of their inadequacy.

Moses. When God appeared to him at the burning bush, Moses hid his face (Ex. 3:1–14). Of course, it was known that no one could see God and live, but could Moses also be thinking, "I'm a murderer; don't see me for who I am"? God's gracious answer turned Moses' words around and, regardless of Moses' fearing being exposed as inadequate, God said, "The whole point is that I will be glorified through an inadequate vessel like you. The deliverance will not be about you; it'll be about me."

Gideon. Gideon's story is similar (Judg. 6:11–24), but it is based on the inadequacy of his family and his being seen among his people as "less than." Of course, we know Gideon's additional Strategy: "Prove your promise. Here's a fleece. Show me for sure." God graciously "performs" in response to Gideon's request (or was it a Demand?). Why couldn't Gideon have been satisfied with God's assurance, "But I will be with you"?

Jeremiah. Jeremiah's Self-Promotion Strategy of Inadequacy is his belief that he is too young and inexperienced (Jer. 1:5–10). But God answered his concerns by supplying him words which equal knowledge and a plan.

We may think that pointing out our inadequacies to God is being humble before him, but consider whether it might be a form of disobedience and rebellion. Could it be that we are resisting God's call because we are trying to protect ourselves from harm of some sort. Maybe we don't want to be seen as inadequate so we tell God he has made a mistake.

Just think. Did Moses really expect God to reply, "Oh, yeah, that's right. Sorry, I forgot that you stutter. Excuse me. I'll go ask someone else." (In his graciousness, he did also call Moses' brother, Aaron, to be his partner and spokesman.)

Or to Gideon: "Oh, yeah, that's right. Sorry, I forgot that folks in your tribe don't respect your clan. Excuse me. I'll go find a true leader."

Or to Jeremiah: "Oh, yeah, that's right. Sorry, I forgot you're young. Excuse me, I'll go get someone older and more experienced."

How ridiculous. Our Strategy is not wisdom or humility. It is a diversionary tactic to make sure we are not put in situations where there is danger. Moses most likely was afraid of humiliation as a stutterer, and he was worried that the Israelites would call him an imposter. Gideon most likely was afraid of contempt for his family. His clan had already been disregarded as "less than" in some way by the rest of his tribe. Jeremiah most likely was afraid that his message might be rejected because of his immaturity and ignorance.

God's graciousness persisted with each man as he gave them assurances of his power, presence, and plans.

Which of those three promises are you choosing to reject and, as a result, are choosing your own Self-Promotion Strategy of Inadequacy? Like Moses, Gideon, and Jeremiah, each of us does it in different and creative ways, but most likely we are responding to God with the same basic Strategies. And that response is motivated by a Vow to not be seen as a liar, less than, immature, ignorant, inadequate, imperfect, and the list goes on and on. Can you identify your own?

The Temperaments

Since as speakers and writers we have taught about the Temperaments for many years, it might seem incongruous that we would call them a Strategy. Although we find great value in identifying ourselves and others through this Temperament method, we also see how such information can become a Strategy that is Self-Promotion and Sinful. Our sin nature may want to take this valuable information and misuse it.

The main danger is that we discover our Temperament and then it becomes our security. We depend upon it for refusing to change and become more like Christ. Or we may believe that God should not allow a trial that requires living outside our Temperament's strengths. But let's first examine the essential descriptions of each Temperament.

There are four basic Temperaments. The system we have used names them thus:

> *Expressive:* a person who is lively, talkative, people oriented, and loves fun.
> *Driver:* a person who wants to be in charge, makes quick decisions, and rarely second-guesses those decisions.
> *Analytical:* loves details, makes slow decisions, and strives for perfection.
> *Amiable:* wants peace at any cost, quiet, slow moving/thinking.

Knowing our Temperament *is* helpful in that we can gain understanding of our personality bents. From birth, babies show tendencies in certain directions. Some babies are lively; some are calmer. Some don't need as much attention; some demand constant attention. Of course, many contributing factors determine who a person becomes, including the elements of the model we are sharing in this book (which we believe is the major contributing factor to our adult reactions). Still, each of us is born with an initial tendency in a certain direction. The problem begins when we depend on our natural inclinations instead of trusting God and being willing to step out of our natural bent.

For instance, the Expressive loves being with people and could be tempted to say, "No, God, don't ask me to sit quietly and spend time at a retreat just with you. That's too hard. I need to be moving." But ask her or him to give the devotional at the retreat on prayer, and they will be glad to teach on it.

Or the Driver who loves to be in charge could be tempted to say, "God, you want me to relinquish control over the meeting of which I'm the leader? That's too hard. I need to make sure things go the way I think they should." But ask him or her to step in at the last minute and tell people what to do and they will be glad to give their opinion.

Or the Analytical who loves perfection could be tempted to say, "God, you can't possibly ask me to be satisfied with relaxing my standards. That's too hard to be associated with imperfection." But ask him or her to step in to correct problems and they will be thrilled.

Or finally, the Amiable who loves peace could be tempted to say, "God, why can't everyone get along? No one should become riled up by things opposed to Bible doctrine. It's too hard to confront someone." But ask them to mediate a disagreement and they will be glad to.

As you can see, we might begin to refuse to trust God if he were to challenge us out of our comfort zone.

Knowledge of the Temperaments can also become a Strategy when we value one temperament more than another and therefore buy into the Strategy of Inadequacy. In Christian circles, the Expressive is highly valued because they seem to be able to talk to anyone and everyone about Christ. They have no trouble or embarrassment. It is possible they are just doing what is natural for them and applying it to the area of evangelism. Of course, it is possible they are using God's power, but Satan could easily tempt them to depend upon their natural bent.

The Amiable, Driver, and Analytical could easily think, "I'm not a very good Christian because I don't speak freely about Jesus like my friend does." The Amiable or any other low-key kind of Temperament could give up even trying to speak about their Christian beliefs because they don't do it "right"—like the Expressive does.

So we have those who criticize others who don't do it like them—whatever it is they do well. And we have others who feel discouraged because they don't do it like someone else—whatever it is that they can't do well. It is good to know our natural bent, but sinful to become proud or discouraged about it.

When we teach about the Temperaments, we talk about the principle of versatility. That means being willing to do what God wants you to do as the Lord leads—and in his power—to do it. We are not being versatile if we refuse to do anything that is outside our natural bent. God may intentionally ask the Expressive to be quiet in order to draw from God's strength to do so. God may intentionally ask the Driver to give up power in order to trust God's sovereign control.

Jesus is the ultimate versatility expert. He chose whichever tendency fit best with the situation. At different times, he used the strengths of each Temperament, and he displayed none of the weaknesses (yes, every Temperament has its own set of weaknesses). Because we have the mind of Christ and we are empowered by the very Spirit of God, we also can choose in God's power to be versatile in the same way, regardless of our Temperament.

How about Those Questions?

Remember the questions you answered in the first chapter? Let's look now at how your answers could point out your own unique Strategies. And remember, the Strategies we covered in these two chapters are only a few of the numerous possibilities. (Some of these we have highlighted before but they can apply to different areas.)

- *What instruction in the Bible do you wish was not there?* That Bible verse could direct you to how you are determined to protect, provide, or promote yourself apart from God.
- *How do you hate being seen by others?* Your answer here could indicate People-Pleasing or other kinds of Self-Promoting Sinful Strategies.
- *If something could be changed in your life, that could make you happy, what would it be?* Your answer here could point you to how something provides what God wants to provide for you.
- *If you could change one person's opinion or perception of you, who would it be and what would it be?* Your answer here could be a strong indication of what you base your image on instead of God's opinion of you in Christ.
- *When you're not happy, what do you do for escape?* This could point to a Strategy to provide for yourself in ways that are a substitute for seeking God.
- *What three things, people, or circumstances bring you the most happiness?* It could be that one

or more of those elements could point to an Idol that feeds a Strategy.

- **Who are you determined not to be like?** Ask yourself, if I become like that person, what will it say about me? That could be a red flag that you need other people's approval instead of God's.
- **Who do you want to be like, aside from Jesus?** Again, ask yourself, if I become like that person, in what ways will I slurp at the broken cistern of finding my identity outside of seeking God's view of me?

Some of those were the questions, I (Larry) asked John as I counseled him about his jealousy of his wife. His wife, Becky, was a professional marriage and family counselor. John explained that he feared his wife was attracted to a particular male client because she seemed to spend extra time with him, and they talked and texted outside of her office, even though it is prohibited.

I asked him, "What does this feel like?"

"Like the plea for attention that I felt as a little boy toward my father. He rarely gave me attention, and he told me everything wrong was my fault. Yet I pursued him, in the sense that I tried to be the perfect boy and teenager. I never received what I longed for."

I was surprised at his ability to quickly see a connection to his past. That was unusual.

He continued, "I think it's like I'm also trying to pursue my wife, yet she doesn't acknowledge it. I thought women wanted to be pursued. That's why her relationship with this man seems so threatening. I keep trying to compete for her attention, but my efforts are not rewarded—just like it was with my father. I'm like a little puppy waiting for attention. Once I realized my father wasn't ever going to give me what I craved, I vowed I'd never beg again for attention. When it seems I'm begging my wife for attention, I hate myself for being so weak."

"Did someone tell you that you were weak?"

"Well, I was considered the wimp of the neighborhood and got beat up a few times."

"How did that make you feel?"

"Like I was out of control. I hated that feeling. Oh! I just thought of something that may be important. My mother and father divorced because the woman who broke up their marriage would stand outside our house and call to my father, 'Come out to me'—and things like that. My mom would just sit and cry. I then vowed I would never let any man steal my wife from me. My mom was weak, and I wasn't going to be. I would take action! But now I realize that any action I take will be ineffective. I'm now out of control and weak too."

John seemed like he was about to cry. I paused to allow him to collect himself, and then asked, "What did it mean to you when you and Becky first dated and married?"

"I was ecstatic. She really seemed to value me. For the first time, I didn't feel like that puppy dog chasing after crumbs. I guess those are mixed metaphors, but that's how I felt."

"Is that good feeling threatened now?"

It seemed like a light bulb came on in John's mind. "That's it, isn't it? She provides me what I've always lacked."

"And how does that leave out God?"

"Well, I don't depend upon his opinion of me. Is that what's going on? Why I feel so threatened?"

"What would being strong in the Lord look like—since God says you're not a wimp?"

John paused to think. "I think it would be telling her calmly how this makes me feel while also telling her how much I love her."

"Have you considered that requiring her to meet your needs has to be intimidating to her? To be required to be someone's provider when only God can be, almost has to make her run away. She knows she's inadequate for that assignment."

"I never thought of it like that. I thought depending on her would help her feel needed."

Within a few more minutes John was ready to pray and repent of putting expectations on his wife that she couldn't meet. Then he surrendered to the point of releasing control over her and wanting to allow God to meet his needs.

I heard from John some time after that, and he gave me an update: "I haven't been able to never get Hooked by the jealousy and fear of that man, but God still worked. It was revealed to Becky that her client had been deceitful. He had always claimed that his wife didn't want to work on their marriage. But somehow the wife found out about Becky counseling him, and she showed up at one of his sessions. When she said she wanted to participate, he left the office angry. Becky sees now that she had been taken in somewhat and was more vulnerable than she thought."

John's story shows how we can so easily succumb to a Self-Protective Strategy. But there is always hope of having a heart change by repenting of the lies. God is strong enough.

Reflections and Group Discussion Questions

1. Of the three basic types of Strategies (Prevent, Provide, and Promote), which do you think you fall into the most?

2. Before reading this chapter, would you have given Isaiah 50:10–11 the same meaning? What would you have described as the meaning before reading this chapter?

3. Did the quote from Dan Allender about Isaiah 50:10–11 give you any insight? If so, what?

4. Did you relate at all to the Strategy of the Victim? If so, how?

5. Have you previously considered favorably the thought, "This too will pass"? What do you think now?

6. What additional insights do you have to share about the passage on the rich young ruler?

7. Did the ideas about that passage offer you any new insights? Do you relate to the rich young ruler?

8. Of these options in the Self-Promote Strategy category, which is most attractive and tempting to you: prominence, power, acclaim, perfection, or praise?

9. Heather Kopp talks about "setting a trap." Can you identify any ways you do the same thing? What are your motives?

10. To what degree do you succumb to the People-Pleasing Strategy? Can you give any example of how that was lived out recently?

11. Did you gain any new insight from studying Moses, Gideon, and Jeremiah in the section about the Self-Promotion Strategy of Inadequacy? Do you respond to God the same way any of them did? What do you want to do differently the next time God invites you into some opportunity?

12. What did you think about the section on the Temperaments?

Section II

The Living Spring

We have come a long way, and it has been hard work. You may be seeing things in a different light. Hopefully, you have begun to see the ways you seek your spiritual nourishment through a broken cistern full of mud or lacking water.

Now we have come to the section that will offer insights for more consistently seeking God's empowering from his living spring.

If you are tempted to read this section before reading the previous chapters, then please resist! This may seem like the "How to Be Holy" section that will bring the relief from pain that you desire, but it doesn't work like that. Without identifying what has come before, we don't know what to resist and what to repent of.

These final three chapters are not going to be just a checklist. We hope in these pages to show you how to live a godly life marked by holiness, surrender, and obedience. But all those things come from the desire to please God because of all that he has done for us. This kind of successful, satisfying living comes from the heart.

Chapter 8

Repentance

A man cannot apply himself seriously to repentance without knowing himself to belong to God.

—John Calvin

Repentance without rejoicing will lead to despair.

—Tim Keller

I have walked with other men through the grief process of losing a wife or a child. I hoped to comfort them by entering into their grief and sharing their pain. I was surprised to see, however, that God might want to use that sad journey to invite them into repentance. That's what happened with Justin.

Within six months of his wife's death, Justin had begun putting his name on dating sites and asking his friends for recommendations. When those friends expressed some hesitation, he was surprised. "I'm just so lonely," he explained. "The hole left in my heart now that Lisa is gone is just unbearable. And remember? Even she said she wanted me to get married again and be happy. She knew I need a wife."

He laughed, trying to lighten the concern of his friends. When one friend asked, "Is that God's will for you?" he eagerly nodded, "Of course! How could it not be?"

That was the background information I had learned from others when I met Justin. His question to me confirmed what I had heard. He asked me, "Do you know of any available godly women?" Justin seemed intrigued when I asked some questions that took the conversation in a different direction. I was impressed when he was willing to continue talking by sharing his story.

I asked Justin about his childhood, and he described deep loneliness while growing up. He was an only child and in his book "only" meant "lonely." He longed for a brother or sister, he said, and he was surprised when I told him I also was an only child but I had never longed for a sibling. "Really?" he replied, "I would have never imagined that was possible."

Then Justin tried to laugh it off when he described how he begged his parents to have another child, and they criticized him for not being content by himself. But that experience did not take away his longings, and when he saw other families with several children, he fantasized about how much fun it would be to have siblings.

A restless loneliness had developed within him, and it was not satisfied until he met and married Lisa in their early twenties. He found in her the solution for his loneliness, and they did everything together. In tears, he described her to me as "my soul mate," as if no one else on earth had ever had such a fulfilling marriage. "When she died, I was crushed," Justin whispered, as he tried to control the sobs that seemed about to erupt within him.

When I wondered aloud whether God might want to fill his loneliness with or without re-marrying, Justin looked at me as if I had slapped him. "There's no way God wouldn't want me to be happy by having a new wife, right?"

That question became the foundation for us meeting together over several weeks. In time, his eyes were opened to see that his childhood without siblings was a kind of Wound from which came the Message: "I'm missing out, and I won't be complete until I have someone to share my life with." That birthed the Vow of "I must never feel lonely," because loneliness made him feel incomplete. Then he could recognize that Lisa had become his Idol, replacing God as his fulfillment. When that Idol was removed and loneliness again loomed dangerously close, Justin became Hooked, which showed itself in the way he frantically tried to find a woman who would keep away the "incomplete" feeling he hated.

Most importantly, as we continued to delve into his sad world, he was willing to acknowledge how he was not choosing God as his source for life, so he took his name off the dating sites he had entered. This helped him to Repent of making human companionship his god rather than Jesus, who promised never to leave or forsake him.

Ultimately, Justin was able to come even to the point of Surrender (the topic of our next chapter) and with tears to pray, "Lord, even if I never marry again, I'll seek to find the solution for my loneliness in you. I want you to meet that need so that I can draw ever closer to you."

Although it was a hard road of Surrendering over and over again, Justin's spiritual walk with Christ deepened to the point that he told me, "I never could have imagined being as close to the Lord as I am now. Of course, I still want to get remarried, but I'm no longer demanding it. I'm resting in whatever God has for me. He knows best."

Like Justin's story, we have shared other true accounts of people who put the pieces together for heart transformation. Think back to some of them.

As I have confessed earlier in this book, I (Kathy) vowed to never be seen as imperfect. My Strategy was perfectionism. I have identified my sin of trying to replace God's plan of salvation with my perfect works, and I have repented of thinking I could become perfect on this earth.

I (Larry) have also told you how I vowed to be in control and never be seen as weak. My Strategy was to be always in control. I have recognized my sin of pushing away God's empowering, and thus I have repented of trying to avoid appearing weak.

Heather (in Chapter Two) vowed to be the source of happiness for others. Her Strategy was People-Pleasing. She saw her sin of replacing God as the source of happiness for her mother and repented of thinking she knew better than God.

Ken (in Chapter Three) vowed to avoid taking responsibility for his choices. His Strategy was to blame his parents for his reactions. He could distinguish that he was rejecting God's conviction, so he repented of refusing God's viewpoint.

Sharon (in Chapter Three) vowed to protect herself from emotional pain. Her Strategy was to bury her feelings. She responded to God's conviction by seeing her sin of not trusting in God's loving plan, and she repented of her anger toward him.

Sam (in Chapter Four) vowed to never allow his failure to be seen. His Strategy was to make sure he received the approval of others. He became honest about his sin of rejecting God's grace and he repented of his pride.

In Chapter Five, I, Larry, vowed to never be out of control. My Strategy was to be critical of other drivers, which made me feel superior and thus gave me a false sense of control. I repented of my arrogance when I saw my Strategy as rebellion against God's sovereignty.

Tricia Goyer (in Chapter Six) vowed to never be in danger again. Her Strategy was to depend upon herself. She recognized her sin of claiming that her way was better than God's and repented of refusing God's care.

We Fall on Our Knees Because of Grace

As we have traveled through the previous chapters of this book, we have begun to see the sinful foundation (Messages, Vows, Strategies) that is the kindling wood for our ungodly reactions (being Hooked). That foundation is fanned by leaving God out of our thinking. By recognizing that choice, we can clearly see that we have dug our own cistern instead of seeking God as our living spring. We are shocked, and most likely relieved, to realize that we don't have to live in the "natural" way but can live supernaturally.

In hindsight, we must admit that our Strategies say something regarding what we think about God.

- God can't be trusted to provide the power for me to choose wisely.
- God is not wise in the way he is handling my life.
- God hates me because he allows bad things to happen to me.
- God is distant and uninvolved because he does not respond the way I think he should.

Isn't that what we are *really* saying?

This is why such responses are sin. Without realizing it at the time, we are blaspheming God by saying lies about him. As we gain insights into why we feel and act the way we do, we begin to understand that our reactions are no longer just some innocuous and benign response that seems expected, normal, and without consequences. No, we are speaking lies about the loving, wise, strong, and caring God of the universe. Our choices and our Strategies are calling God names, incorrect names. And we should be horrified. It should humble us so that we will acknowledge our sin.

We can take a lesson from Isaiah. After hearing God described by the seraphim singing, "Holy, holy, holy is the LORD of hosts; the whole earth is full of his glory!" Isaiah cries out, "Woe is me! For I am lost; for I am a man of unclean lips, and I dwell in the midst of a people of unclean lips; for my eyes have seen the King, the LORD of hosts!" (Isa. 6:3–5).

But when, like Isaiah, we see how good and upright and almighty God really is, then we realize and are amazed that we aren't destroyed by this holy and perfect God. We should be, but we are not. We should be destroyed in retaliation for misrepresenting him. We are trying to tear down his character. He is holy and we are not. Yet, we are not given the consequences we deserve. From heaven we receive grace. That is the meaning of Romans 2:4: "Do you presume on the riches of his kindness and forbearance and patience, not knowing that God's kindness is meant to lead you to repentance?"

And all of this happens to us because of God's loving grace and his gift of redemption through Jesus Christ. Like Isaiah, we receive what we need—forgiveness and cleansing. Remember what happened to Isaiah? "Then one of the seraphim flew to me, having in his hand a burning coal that he had taken with tongs from the altar. And he touched my mouth and said: 'Behold, this has touched your lips; your guilt is taken away, and your sin atoned for'" (Isa. 6:6–7).

For us who are Christians that burning coal represents the cleansing Jesus provides through his shed blood on the cross. Because of that sacrifice, grace provides forgiveness and cleansing that result in our being declared righteous. This is the gospel. The grace offered in the gospel is the good news that even though we all deserve to be wiped out because of our sin, God sent Jesus to die for us on the cross. His act of love makes it possible for his chosen child to receive forgiveness and cleansing. It has nothing to do with our being good enough or doing things right. It is a gift (Eph. 2:8–9).

And because of this amazing gift, we should respond as Isaiah did when he heard the Lord asking, "Whom shall I send, and who will go for us?" Do you remember Isaiah's answer? He said, "Here I am! Send me'" (Isa. 6:8). So should we.

Like Isaiah, though, we should not respond in obedience because we think we are earning the grace and mercy. We respond in obedience because we are so grateful for it. Because of that gratitude, we love Christ more and more. Because of that grateful love, we desire to turn from those Sinful Strategies. This turning away, which is repentance, ultimately changes the motives of our hearts. Now we want to cooperate with the Holy Spirit. And we become more willing to surrender to a newer more powerful affection: being a child of God. The Puritan writer Thomas Chalmers called it "the expulsive power of a new affection." Our gratitude responds in Surrender to obey whatever God has for us, even though it feels dangerous. In our next chapter, we will examine the topic of Surrender more fully. And then in our final chapter, we will look more closely at that new affection.

Not a One-Time Thing

Our Repentance is needed both at our point of salvation and every day after that. Every day we depend upon that gospel because we fail every day. We don't repent repeatedly in order to be saved again and again, but to be able to abide in Christ.

When I was a little girl, I believed God was the kind of god who held an ax over my head, just waiting for me to do something wrong so that he could punish me. I kept track in my mind of my good deeds and my bad deeds, hoping against hope that there would be more good deeds than bad deeds when I died. I didn't have a sense of God's kindness and love. I truly believed I had to earn my way into heaven—even to the point of becoming perfect.

When I received Christ as my Lord and Savior at the age of eighteen with my boyfriend, Larry, sitting beside me in the pastor's office, I was amazed that I had just heard that God didn't have an ax or a scale. I could not earn my way. God offered what I needed as a free gift, the gospel of grace.

In response to that offer, I felt a gratitude that overwhelmed me to the point of tears. I knew I deserved the ultimate penalty of death, and yet I had just heard that I could apply the gospel to me. What glorious news! What freedom! And I wanted to please God because I was so grateful for his gift.

Since then, I have been learning to apply that same truth to my everyday living: being so grateful for God's gracious work in me that I want to obey. That is my desire even though I miss the mark every day. But praise God! His grace covers that also.

What Repentance Is Not

Even though Repentance is available and we need it, we still try to steer clear of it. It is a scary word. It sounds old-fashioned and stilted. But to tell you the truth, we just can't find a better word for what is involved in heart transformation. Repentance, that uncomfortable word, is what we need when we are faced with our Strategies. Unfortunately, a lot of misconceptions plant confusion about Repentance, such as thinking that it requires self-contempt. We may think we must beat ourselves over the head mentally and emotionally to show God how sorry we are before we can be forgiven and cleansed.

But Repentance does not require self-contempt. Repentance actually involves humility, and it creates humility. Psalm 51 is the great chapter of King David's repentance for his horrific sins of adultery, murder, and the subsequent cover-up. Deep repentance can be detected in David's words, but they contain no self-contempt. Verses 1–2 set the tone:

> Have mercy on me, O God,
>   according to your steadfast love;
> according to your abundant mercy
>   blot out my transgressions.
> Wash me thoroughly from my iniquity,
>   and cleanse me from my sin!

David does not even start his psalm by concentrating on his own wickedness, other than to mention it. Instead, the whole psalm focuses on God and the hope he provides because of his gracious love and mercy.

Let's look at the difference between Self-Contempt, which creates a false Repentance, and Humility, which creates a true Repentance.

Self contempt	Humility
Believing I'm stupid	Believing I'm undone
Wanting to hide	Wanting my sin revealed
Feeling hopeless	Believing there is hope through forgiveness and cleansing
Sad I got caught	Glad I got caught
I'm helpless	God's power is available to me
I turn my face away from God in shame	I turn to God and claim Jesus' righteousness
I have to earn my way back into God's favor	I'm grateful for grace that receives me through Jesus' death and resurrection
I'm condemned and will give up	I'm convicted, but there's a way back
God is punishing me	God is training me for future godliness

Repentance is also not regret—at least, not the wrong kind of regret. Let's look at that difference. You'll notice there are some elements in common with Self-contempt and Humility.

Regret	Repentance
Focuses on outward behavior	Focuses on my heart motives
Sorry I got caught	Glad I got caught
Motivated by the pain of consequences	Motivated by desiring relationship with God
Wants to hide sin and resists asking for forgiveness	Takes responsibility for my own sin and asks for forgiveness
Only changes enough for the appearance of image	Continues to examine life and be honest
Downplays the sin	Fully admits the sin
Embarrassed because image is marred	Grieved for the pain sin caused others
Leaves open the door for further sinning	Seeks the Spirit's full power for change

There is a godly regret that we call "godly sorrow," and we will talk about that later. For the most part Satan takes regret and tries to twist it into something that lacks grace. But God intended regret to be like Repentance in turning us to the cross for forgiveness and cleansing. The plan was to have it operate like a temperature gauge on a car. That gauge tells us when something is wrong and needs to be addressed. Likewise, when we regret a choice, we should allow the Holy Spirit to draw us into a humble Repentance dependent upon the cleansing from Jesus' death on the cross.

What Is Repentance?

Repentance is a turning away from one direction (toward sin) and going in a different direction (toward holiness). Technically, the word in the New Testament means "change your mind." But it is not just the changing of one idea, or even a few; it is a radical change in the whole direction a person is traveling—spiritually, mentally, and emotionally. Repentance won't bring perfection or a lack of temptation, but it reorients the desires within the penitent person. God is supposed to be our source of motivation and power, yet our desires to have our own way lure us to dig our own sinful cistern of polluted water and try to convince us that it tastes good.

To come to the point of Repentance, we must call sin *sin*. We must accept the fact that what we are doing or feeling about the situation in question is not just some innocuous way to respond to life but it is sin, because it is based on a Strategy. It is sin not only because we are leaving out God, but because we are actually turning against him. It is sin not just because it is distasteful but because it is horrible. These responses of Repentance—to that degree—may not occur all the time, but the penitent person has decided, "I don't want to grieve God's heart like this anymore and kick mud on his holiness." If we claim he is Lord and yet we are cooperating with a Strategy, we are telling him he is not worthy to be followed. Repentance acknowledges this mudslinging as sin; it wants to turn away from it and walk toward Surrender based on gratitude for all God has done for us.

It is an incredible experience when we see Repentance occur in the lives of others (and ourselves). Grant came to that point. Grant and his fiancée Julie met with us because Julie was complaining about Grant's pervasive pessimism. Nothing pleased him. He was critical of everything. Julie was so weary of it that she was thinking of giving back his ring. As we asked questions about his negativity, Grant defended himself. "Hey, I'm just being cautious. Too many bad things happen in this life." Although we also could have delved into Julie's need to control his pessimism, we started with Grant.

Through several conversations, he began identifying how both a Message and a Vow were connected to his need to be pessimistic. As a child, he was touched sexually by an uncle. Typical of sex-abuse victims, he became Hypervigilant to try to keep the abuse from occurring again. The Message he agreed with was: "I can never be a true man because I wasn't able to protect myself." His Vow became, "I will push everyone away through negativity to limit exposure to possible danger. I can't risk someone seeing me as not man enough to protect myself." Of course, he was not aware that all of this was occurring. But as we heard his history of breaking off relationships, the pattern became more apparent—even to him.

When Grant saw how he was protecting himself rather than trusting God, he couldn't stop the tears. "I've never seen it this way before. I just thought it was a good way to be. I really don't want to distrust God. I've always thought I did trust God and his love for me. But now I can see how much I've tried to be in control."

He turned to Julie and said, "Oh, honey, I'm so sorry. I can see how I've made your life miserable. Please forgive me."

Julie was thrilled and kissed him.

Grant continued, "I want to ask God to forgive me. I'm going to pray right now, okay?"

Of course we nodded, even as we also brushed away tears.

Grant prayed, "Precious Lord, I am so sorry. I deceived myself into thinking I was doing what you wanted me to do. I can see now that I was actually protecting myself instead of putting my care into your hands. Forgive me and cleanse me. I really don't want to be like this. Thank you, Father God."

Of course, Grant's Repentance would not quickly brush away all his bad habits, but it was an important first step. And eventually he also came to the place of forgiving that abusive uncle. Though his uncle was deceased, Grant wrote him a letter and then burned it in a forgiveness ceremony.

Grant was willing to move into Repentance because he saw his Strategies as sin in the sight of God, especially in light of God's perfect holiness. No longer was his sin just a harmless reaction but actually a commentary about who he believed God is. His quick Repentance was unusual, but he made a distinct connection between his protective behavior and his rebellion. Not everyone grasps this right away.

For true Repentance, we need to take God's holiness seriously.

Take God's Holiness Seriously

Taking God's holiness seriously is the point of the biblical story of Uzzah—a story that reveals the shaky ground of doing otherwise.

Here is what happened. The ark of the covenant was the literal representation and abiding place of God's holy Presence. For some time, it had been in the Philistines' camp because the Israelites had been defeated in battle (1 Sam. 4). When the Philistines began getting sick, the ark was blamed and they wanted to give it back. That's when it was transferred to the Israelites on a cart. Many years passed, during which even the Israelites suffered severe repercussions when they mishandled the Holy Ark. For over twenty years, during the rule of Samuel, it was faithfully and respectfully housed in ancient Hebron. Finally, when David became king of all Israel and established Jerusalem as his fortress/capital, he decided to move the ark to what would become Israel's holy city. This "man after God's own heart" carefully planned the ark's transfer to Jerusalem. He built a brand new cart to haul it and planned an elaborate procession of priests and soldiers to accompany it.

Second Samuel 6:6–7 tells us what happened next. "When they came to the threshing floor of Nacon, Uzzah put out his hand to the ark of God and took hold of it, for the oxen stumbled. And the anger of the LORD was kindled against Uzzah, and God struck him down there because of his error, and he died there beside the ark of God."

At a first reading, we might feel a little miffed at God. Wasn't Uzzah just responding in careful concern for the well-being of the ark? Why would God react so severely? This was exactly David's first reaction to Uzzah's death, before the king thought it over and humbled himself in fear before the Almighty.

Uzzah most likely was a Kohathite, a family branch of the Levites who were trained to transport the ark by carrying it with long poles inserted into the rings built into the ark. They were not allowed to touch the ark at the cost of death (Num.

4:15) because it was God's holy dwelling place. This warning reveals the extent of God's holiness. Any person touching the ark was basically claiming equality with God. In effect, that is what any sin says.

Uzzah should have made sure the ark was transported the godly way. When it seemed the ark would fall, Uzzah most likely thought he should "rescue" the ark from damage, destruction or becoming sullied by dirt. Yet the earth always obeys God. Only man rebels against God's holy rule over his life.

We do not know Uzzah's heart condition, but his behavior could indicate that he had some pride about his position. Was his Strategy, "I want to look good taking care of the ark; I don't want anyone to see me as incompetent"? Unfortunately, he made his sinful choice, and God took his life. (We were inspired for some of our thoughts on Uzzah by R. C. Sproul in his book, *The Holiness of God*, accessed on Kindle.)

Such insights should bring us to Repentance as we honestly agree with a serious and healthy viewpoint of God's incredible holiness. If we see how much we lack standing before a perfect God, we will be more willing to repent.

We have already looked at Psalm 51, but here is an important insight from King David. He writes, "I know my transgressions, and my sin is ever before me. Against you, you only, have I sinned and done what is evil in your sight, so that you may be justified in your words and blameless in your judgment" (verses 3–4). As deeply as he hurt individuals and the whole community of Israelites, his real sin still was against God. This speaks of the seriousness of his slander of God's holiness.

Such a deep awareness like David's is not something we can force ourselves to sense, but we can pray, asking God to make these truths real to our hearts.

Preventing a Hardened Heart

Without that serious and healthy viewpoint of God's holiness (and our lack thereof), we can easily slip into a hardened heart. Earlier we wrote about Romans 2:4 and its important role in bringing us to Repentance. Paul asks here, "Do you presume on the riches of his kindness and forbearance and patience, not knowing that God's kindness is meant to lead you to repentance?"

The verse that follows tells us: "But because of your hard and impenitent heart you are storing up wrath for yourself on the day of wrath when God's righteous judgment will be revealed."

If we don't respond to the kindness God provides through the gospel, we will end up with a hardened heart. Let's look at two insights that will help us reject a hardened heart so that we can respond to God's kindness, forbearance, and patience.

Railroad Tracks Syndrome

Remember Grant whose Strategy was pessimism? As he shared his childhood stories and talked about his reactions, he inadvertently called attention to what we call Railroad Tracks syndrome. This is when we say we believe one thing (usually the biblical, godly way) but our behavior reveals the opposite. Our claim of obedience is one of the rails on that railroad track, and in this metaphor we think we are living a "monorail" life. But the truth is, we are on a railroad track with two rails! And the other rail is the opposite of what we claim.

For instance, in Grant's life he said he trusted God totally, but his need to be pessimistic proved he was more often trusting his own schemes instead. He pushed people away to make sure friendships didn't create pain. But he truly thought he was trusting God. As a result, he would not face his sin and, of course, then he couldn't repent.

Having Railroad-Tracks thinking prevents Repentance, because we really don't see that there is anything to repent of!

Let's listen to some actual comments we have heard:

"Of course I trust God; but it's no big deal for me to worry a little about something this important." *The truth:* God says, "Do not be anxious about *anything*" (Phil. 4:6–7, emphasis added).

"Of course, I love my husband; but the only way he'll be motivated to clean up the yard is if I nag him a little." *The truth:* God says, "Do all things without grumbling or disputing" (Phil. 2:14).

"Of course, I have God's power to do whatever he wants me to do; but I'm not so sure I could be a missionary to some third-world country." *The truth:* God says, "I can do all things through him who strengthens me" (Phil. 4:13).

Author and businessman Dave Goetz gives us an example of the Railroad Tracks syndrome.

> On a fly-fishing trip, with still an hour in the truck before arriving home, my fishing buddy off-handedly observed that I was overly sensitive to criticism. He listed a couple instances, including my response to some reviews of my writing. Suddenly, the truck felt cramped. I snapped back that simply debating what others say about me or what I do isn't being overly sensitive. I asked him to give more specific examples, which I debunked. Hurt, I withdrew from the conversation and nursed my new wound from a friend. How could I be sensitive to criticism?

Do you see his Railroad Tracks syndrome? Goetz responded to criticism by being overly sensitive to his friend's comment that he was overly sensitive. And finally he said, "How could *I* be sensitive to criticism?" This just was not his view of himself. In effect, he said, "I'm not overly sensitive, but don't criticize me, because I'm going to be overly sensitive."

We all have this syndrome in our lives, and it deceives us and keeps us from being aware of our sins. As a result, we develop a hardened heart that becomes resistant to Repentance.

Recognizing our own Railroad Tracks thinking most often requires the insights of others or maybe of a book like this. Most of the time we are blinded to our inconsistencies because we are thinking that we are right. Being open to repenting means you will have a teachable heart that hears and considers the opinions of others. God may indeed want to use friends and family to help you see your blind spots. Listening to those who love us may also be a way of showing honor to some of his image bearers. Are you willing to do that? Does your gratitude for the grace you have received motivate you to risk and face all that God wants you to face?

Sit in It

A concept that we have found quite enlightening for discovering our hardened hearts is "Sit in It." We can use this tool when we wonder if something is a Strategy that we need to repent from. There are two options for putting this into action.

First, continue to do a particular behavior and pay attention to what it provides to you emotionally. You may notice that you seem to be receiving the fulfillment of your Idol or your Vow, which then supports a Strategy.

Secondly, consciously stop the behavior and pay attention to what you feel you are lacking. You may notice that you seem to be missing the fulfillment of your Idol or what you Vowed. In this case the Strategy is not working.

I remember with great joy when our daughter, Darcy, announced she was engaged. In a short time Kathy and Darcy starting making plans, and, being a male creature, I was surprised by all the required details. Every day something needed to be decided. I didn't have any opinions *yet*. After all, it was not in my circle of interest, so I just stepped back and let the ladies roll.

I already knew how most things in life should happen; read that: *my way*. I knew I would have strong opinions about this event. But deep in my spirit I was struggling. Would my opinions really be that helpful? Was my willingness to share my opinions so freely doing something for me that somehow left out God? I believed that God might be inviting me to "sit in" this whole planning event by uncharacteristically not offering my opinion about any aspect of the wedding. I wanted to be faithful to this call and announced to my daughter that I would not offer any advice. I told her that between her mother, her close friends, and her own desires she would have ample resources to pull everything together.

As the wedding got closer, the pressure seemed to ramp up. Darcy would say, "What do you think, Dad?" This was repeated so often that Kathy or Darcy might ask me a question and answer it with, "That's right, you have no opinion."

Two things happened. First, inside, I got in touch with my desire to offer my overly inflated opinion. This experience exposed my demand to be recognized and to look good. It was humbling. Secondly, my Strategy was exposed as sin, and I repented of trying to control. As a result, freedom started to reign in my life as I merely replied, "I have no opinion."

I maintained this posture until the wedding. Then I was surprised with one other benefit. Having no opinion took the pressure off. All I had to do was show up for one of the most thrilling days of my life, Darcy's wedding.

I (Kathy) also used this tool to examine why I felt compelled to be overly friendly toward service providers, such as a waitress. I sensed that my reaction was extreme, but I felt nervous even thinking of changing it. So I incorporated "sitting in it."

The next time I was in a restaurant, I reacted in my usual way. I smiled. I gushed. I complimented the waitress's pretty hairstyle. And I silently prayed, "Lord, what does my need to do this mean?" I thought I had some ideas, but I wanted to confirm it.

Within a few days, we were out to eat again. This time I took the opposite approach. I didn't smile, and I ordered without even looking at the waitress. And it made me feel so uneasy. I felt tense. I silently prayed, "Lord, what's the meaning of this tension? What's really going on inside me?"

As I literally "sat" there both times, the Holy Spirit gave me the same message: I felt responsible for the waitress's happiness. Something inside me reasoned that if I wasn't extremely friendly and encouraging, the waitress would think I didn't like the food and then feel bad. It boiled down to believing I had power over her emotions, and if she felt bad, then that reflected on me—I was not a very nice person.

In fact, being seen as caring made me feel self-righteous. Finally, I had found something I could do perfectly: be caring. In that way I could control what this waitress thought of me. And I wanted her to smile back to indicate she was enjoying my presence. It was all about me. I didn't really want *her* best. I wanted *my* image to shine.

This may not seem like a big deal, but I struggle with the Idol of People-Pleasing. I believe God cannot be powerful enough to provide the needs of another person. I must be the provider. But playing god is a sin, because when I do it, I am saying that God is not capable of providing what someone else needs.

As a result of sitting in it, I gave the Holy Spirit an opportunity to show me an area where I needed to Repent. I prayed, "Lord, I'm so sorry. I have made something good to be all about me. Even if this waitress thinks poorly of me, I'm still not responsible for her reaction or how she feels about herself. You can provide what she needs. I Repent again in this area of People-Pleasing. Please forgive me. I'm so grateful that you are cleansing me of more and more layers of sin. I'm humbled by your gracious forgiveness and love. Thank you, my Lord."

When I did Repent, a burden fell off my shoulders. I could let God be God in that person's life. Why did I think I could handle someone else's life when I could barely handle my own? I praised God for loving me enough to not let me continue in my sin.

The Hope in Repentance

Does it seem too outrageous to think positively of Repentance? If we can see the hope that Repentance is wrapped in, we can agree with Joe Thorn's thoughts in his book, *Note to Self: The Discipline of Preaching to Yourself.* He explains,

> You need to remember your sins for what they are—
> lawlessness that stemmed from a heart that hated
> God. It wasn't just what you did; it was what you were.
> And in remembering these sins, you hold fast to Jesus.
> This remembrance does not encourage you to shrink

back from God but to draw near, seeking him because of the hope of the gospel. When you remember your sins, you learn humility, love Jesus, and make much of the gospel.

If only we could see the beauty, freedom, encouragement, and joy of Repentance. We are set free and we glorify God. Repentance does not have to be a dirty word! It is God's declaration of grace.

The biblical character Job shows us this freedom and joy. Remember his example of Repentance? After all his children are killed, his wife encourages him to reject God, his friends fail him, and all his earthly resources are gone, Job struggles with wanting to be vindicated as righteous. When God finally answers his pleas to be given an audience, God does not give him what he demands but instead calls Job to acknowledge God's holiness.

Job finally gets it and says, "Behold, I am of small account; what shall I answer you? I lay my hand on my mouth. I have spoken once, and I will not answer; twice, but I will proceed no further" (Job 40:3–5).

Job's words are the words of Repentance. He:

- recognizes he is insignificant. There is nothing of himself that merits acceptance from God.
- recognizes that words are insufficient to defend himself before the sinless, perfect, holy God.
- carries out a submissive act (covering his mouth).
- acknowledges that he had tried to defend himself and it was futile.
- commits to no longer try to protect himself from God's supremacy in his life.

What would your demeanor be while saying those words? Would you be close to tears? Would you hang your head? Or would you look confidently at the Lord who loves you?

Someday you *will* look at Jesus himself, and he will smile and open his arms wide to gather you in. Because your sins have been forgiven and your life has become eternal.

Does thinking of having a similar response bring you fear or hope? Discouragement or anticipation?

Matthew Woodley experienced the joy of Repentance after recognizing his Strategies. But only through God's discipline and invitation to pain. In 2001, he and his family moved to Long Island, New York, hoping to impact the world through pastoring a church. He writes, "I was full of nifty answers to nearly every problem—and honestly, I was also full of myself."

Within a few years, his world had fallen apart. The church suffered from conflict, his wife was diagnosed with cancer, the community remained in shock from 9/11, and he was emptied.

"I didn't know it at the time, but God was taking me on a long, slow journey into brokenness—into the realization that, whatever I am, I'm not whole; I am flawed, vulnerable, and tainted by sin. Coming to this acknowledgment was and still is the best journey I've ever taken."

Matthew writes in a *Discipleship Journal* article about how he became humbled in the midst of his pain. Even though he prayed for the pain to end—quickly—God had other plans. He writes,

> Early in my life I developed my own sophisticated
> (and largely undetected) strategies to hide my broken
> place. Something deep in me thought, *I don't want*
> *you to see parts of my real self: the incompetent,*

aching, angry, and lustful sinner. So I'll artfully present my false self: the super-nice, efficient, spiritually intact pastor. Like an open wound, my brokenness seemed too messy and ugly to reveal. In my fear and shame I started to isolate myself.

After all, what if others discovered the real me? What if they saw the embarrassing pile of shattered pieces in my life? As I scrambled to glue myself back together, my lifestyle kept suggesting, 'Hey, everybody, I'm okay. Really! Give me a few weeks and I'll be like new again.'

But I just couldn't keep it up. So God brought me to the end of my own efforts.

I was learning that this life, which felt like a death, was actually leading me into the power of Christ. Now I'm experiencing God's surprising gifts on a daily basis.

Reflections and Group Discussion Questions

1. Before reading this chapter, what were your opinion and feelings about Repentance?

2. Look again at the four things our Strategies say about God and pick at least one that you identify as something you need to repent of (or come up with your own):

    • God cannot be trusted to provide the power for me to choose wisely.
    • God is not wise in the way he is handling my life.
    • God hates me because he allows bad things to happen to me.
    • God is distant and uninvolved because he does not respond the way I think he should.

3. Does it seem too extreme to say that we are saying lies about God's name through our Strategies? Explain your answer.

4. What impresses you the most from the story of Isaiah (6:3–6)?

5. Share briefly your own story of salvation.

6. From the section "What Repentance Is Not," which concept was new to you or most meaningful to you?

7. What has been your understanding or your standard definition of Repentance? Has your definition of Repentance or your ideas about it changed from reading this chapter?

8. How is the story of Uzzah important to you?

9. Do you think you take God's holiness seriously?

10. How would you encourage someone to take God's holiness seriously?

11. Why is it necessary to have both a healthy and a serious view of God's holiness?

12. Can you see any evidence of the Railroad Tracks syndrome in your life right now?

13. How would you like to use the "Sit in It" concept?

Chapter 9

Surrender

Before we can pray, "Lord, Thy Kingdom come,"
we must be willing to pray,
"My Kingdom go."

—Alan Redpath

The only way God can show us he's in control
is to put us in situations we can't control.

—Unknown

When Tullian Tchividjian moved to Florida to pastor at a new church plant, he and his family were excited. He knew the challenges would be great, but he did not expect it to be as difficult as it could have been if he were returning to an area that was unfamiliar. It was very familiar. In fact, he had grown up in that area of southern Florida, and his parents were well known and respected there. His mother, a nationally known Christian speaker and author, is the daughter of evangelist Billy Graham. His father is a psychologist who has a successful practice.

But after Tullian re-established himself in the area, things fell apart. His father called to tell him his parents were separating after forty-one years of marriage. As Tullian processed this information, he was surprised at how God used it to reveal Idols and Strategies within his life.

"I had told myself that as long as I was their son, I was someone," he confides. "So when they announced their separation, it flipped my world upside down. I began to question everything; who I was, what I'd been taught, even the validity of their faith."

Tullian had depended on his human identity and connections for his power, instead of depending on God to the degree he could have. He continues,

> Anything that we build our lives on, anything that we lean on for meaning or identity, anything that we hope will bring us freedom can be an idol. One of my idols at that point in my life was my family's reputation and the stability of my parents' marriage and faith. The grief brought me to my knees and put me in touch with my need for God in a way that nothing else could have at that moment.
>
> Yet prayer and repentance were not my immediate response. Stubborn sinner that I am, it took a little while to get there. Whenever what we've depended on for meaning—and it's usually one of God's good gifts—is stripped away, our first reaction tends to be one of anger, self-pity, blame, and entitlement. But idolatry feeds on itself, robbing us of joy until we have no other choice but to cry out for God. Fortunately, as one friend puts it, God's office is at the end of your rope.

When Tullian reached the end of his rope, he surrendered to God after repenting of his Idolatry and Self-Promoting Sinful Strategy.

This is what God desires for all of us. Whether or not we fully can identify our Wound, Message, Vow, and Strategy, God desires our good through our Repentance, which leads to Surrender.

What Is Surrender?

Surrender, in the way that we use it here, can be best expressed in two basic ways:

- ***"Even if I'm seen*** in the way I've vowed I'll never be seen, I Surrender to allowing whatever God wants to do with how I'm perceived. I trust that God wants my best, even if I am embarrassed, exposed, and even shamed."
- ***"Even if something occurs*** that my Strategy is designed to prevent, I Surrender, trusting that God knows what he's doing in allowing it."

We find the heart of "even if" in the biblical book of Habakkuk. Habakkuk, the prophet who declared God's judgment to disobedient Israelites, came to that point of Surrender. God had told him that he would use the Assyrians, who were far more wicked than the Israelites, to bring his people into submission. Initially this did not seem like a wise plan to Habakkuk, but after wrestling with it, he surrendered to God's plan and depended on God's wisdom, power, and goodness. Here is the prophet's statement of Surrender:

> I heard and my heart pounded,
>   my lips quivered at the sound;
> decay crept into my bones,
>   and my legs trembled.

Yet I will wait patiently for the day of calamity
    to come on the nation invading us.
Though the fig tree does not bud
    and there are no grapes on the vines,
though the olive crop fails
    and the fields produce no food,
though there are no sheep in the pen
    and no cattle in the stalls,
yet I will rejoice in the LORD,
    I will be joyful in God my Savior.
The Sovereign LORD is my strength;
    he makes my feet like the feet of a deer,
    he enables me to tread on the heights
        (Hab. 3:16–19 NIV, emphasis mine).

What an incredible song of Surrender. Do you see the "even if
. . ." of Surrender? Habakkuk uses a similar idea, "Though . . ."
Though there is no blossoming, fruit, produce, food, flocks, and
herd—all the things Israel needs to survive—Habakkuk says,
"Yet, will I rejoice in God, the LORD who is my strength. Even
though destruction will come, I trust God because he is the
Sovereign LORD. And now let's sing!"

The idea of sovereignty (verse 19) is vital both here and in
our lives. Pastor and author Charles Swindoll defines God's sovereignty as "our all-wise, all-knowing God reigning in realms
beyond our comprehension to bring about a plan beyond our
ability to alter, hinder, or stop."

The same Surrender based in trust of God's sovereignty is
what we desire for you and for ourselves when we encourage us
all to say, "Even if . . ." That Surrender is based on God's qualities
such as wisdom, love, goodness, and sovereignty. Here's a way

to focus on the qualities of our Lord which will empower us to Surrender. It was written by Adam Clarke (1762–1832), a British Methodist theologian.

> [God is] the eternal, independent, and self existent Being; the Being whose purposes and actions spring from himself, without foreign motive or influence; he who is absolute in dominion; the most pure, the most simple, the most spiritual of all essences; infinitely perfect; and eternally self-sufficient, needing nothing that he has made; illimitable in his immensity, inconceivable in his mode of existence, and indescribable in his essence; known fully only by himself, because infinite mind can only be fully comprehended by itself. In a word, a Being who, from his infinite wisdom, cannot err or be deceived, and from his infinite goodness, can do nothing but what is eternally just, and right, and kind.

Having such a perspective can bring us to the point of "Even if" and "Though" despite the presence of our well-worn Strategies, if we are willing to admit each Strategy's sinfulness.

Let us give you some examples. They will seem familiar, yet we now have added the aspect of Surrender.

As I have confessed to you earlier, I (Kathy) Vowed to never be seen as imperfect. My Strategy was perfectionism. I have recognized and Repented of my sin of thinking that I could become perfect and replace God's plan for salvation. Now I am willing to allow people to see my imperfections without trying to defend myself. I have Surrendered to trusting that God will use even my mistakes for his glory and for my good.

As I also have confided to you, I (Larry) Vowed to be in control and never be seen as weak. My Strategy was always to be in control. I have identified my sin and Repented by consciously choosing to listen to other people without trying to correct or persuade them of my perspective. I have Surrendered to allowing things to be out of control at times and waiting to see how God then shows up. I have given up trying to be God; I did a bad job of that. A very bad job.

Heather (in Chapter Two) Vowed to be the source of happiness for others. Her Strategy was People-Pleasing. She saw her sin of trying to be her mom's "Provision" and Repented by at times even refusing to rescue her mom from her problems. She Surrendered to allowing God to work however he wanted to in her mother's life.

Ken (in Chapter Three) Vowed to avoid taking responsibility for his choices. His Strategy was to blame his parents for his reactions. He Repented of rejecting God's conviction. He Surrendered to being honest about his issues so that God could work in him.

Sharon (in Chapter Three) Vowed to protect herself from emotional pain. Her Strategy was to bury her feelings. She Repented from her anger toward God. She Surrendered to allowing God to give her passion for him by being in touch with her feelings.

Sam (in Chapter Four) Vowed to never allow his failure to be seen. His Strategy was to make sure he received the approval of others. He Repented of rejecting God's grace. He Surrendered to allowing his failures to be seen.

In Chapter Five, I, Larry, vowed to never be out of control. My Strategy was to be critical of other drivers, which made me feel superior and thus gave me a false sense of control. I repented of my arrogance when I saw my Strategy as rebellion against God's sovereignty. I Surrendered to seeing these traffic interruptions as God's invitation to trust him in all things.

Tricia Goyer (in Chapter Six) Vowed to never be in danger again. Her Strategy was to depend upon herself. She Repented of refusing God's care. She Surrendered to taking a risk if that was God's desire.

Pamela is currently going through chemotherapy for cancer. She is often nauseous and weak, sleeping much of the time. As a result, she can't fulfill her obligations and be the strong person she has Vowed to be. Pamela had found her meaning in her "Wonder Woman" identity but now recognizes that she was depending not upon God, but only herself. After Repenting of her sin, she is more often saying, "Even if I am seen as weak, I trust God knows what he's doing through this time of trial."

Jarrod loved attending his son Marty's football games because Marty was the star quarterback. In their small town, Jarrod loved the attention he received from being Marty's father. Jarrod never could achieve the skills he longed for in his own high school, so Marty's athleticism filled Jarrod's sails and gave him a sense of fulfillment. But that was before Marty suffered a serious concussion during a game and now his doctors say it might be too dangerous for him to play.

Faced with Marty's removal from sports, Jarrod became nervous and angry. When he realized he was on the verge of insisting that Marty play and thus risking his own son's safety, he was shocked to see his Strategy of needing his son's accomplishments for his own image. After Repenting of his selfishness, Jarrod often tells himself, "Even if Marty can't play again and even if he can, I will find my value in God's opinion of me, not in what other people think or say."

Kendra and Allan are estranged from their son, Julian. Julian blames his parents for his problems because of how they dealt with his learning disability. Even though Kendra and Allan invested thousands of dollars on a variety of therapies and tutors, Julian doesn't acknowledge it. In his mind they chose the wrong help. Kendra and Allan often tell each other, "When Julian sees how much we did for him, then we'll be vindicated." But as time has passed, their perspective has changed. Now they remind each other, "Even if Julian never gives us the gratitude we long for, we thank the Lord for giving us our son. We are learning to look to God for his approval, not to Julian's acknowledgment."

Fruits of Surrender

What will it look like for you as you come to the point of Surrender—when you say, "Even if . . ." and "Though . . ."?

Godly Sorrow

As we have seen God work in our lives and in the lives of others, we have learned that one of the most important and significant fruits of Surrender is Godly Sorrow.

Godly Sorrow is when we grieve about how someone is suffering the effects of their sinful choices, rather than defending our own ungodly behavior as a justified response to them. We begin to desire their Repentance, even if we are never justified, vindicated, and credited with loving them well. And Godly Sorrow most often includes giving grace and mercy to a person who does not deserve it. This response is godly because it is not about us; it is about God being glorified when we treat them with God's kind of love, forgiveness, and understanding.

Of course, Jesus is our perfect example of Godly Sorrow. See his heart in the interaction with the Pharisees and a man with a withered hand:

> Again he entered the synagogue, and a man was there with a withered hand. And they watched Jesus, to see whether he would heal him on the Sabbath, so that they might accuse him. And he said to the man with the withered hand, "Come here." And he said to them, "Is it lawful on the Sabbath to do good or to do harm, to save life or to kill?" But they were silent. And he looked around at them with anger, grieved at their hardness of heart, and said to the man, "Stretch out your hand." He stretched it out, and his hand was restored. The Pharisees went out and immediately held counsel with the Herodians against him, how to destroy him (Mark 3:1–6).

Jesus models for us Godly Sorrow and Righteous Indignation. Jesus was angry, and his anger was aroused by the Pharisees' "hardness of heart." He longed for them to enjoy a true relationship with their heavenly Father instead of the painful consequences of hard hearts. And he longed for them to enjoy the fruits of godly compassion for a hurting man. Jesus' anger was not sinful, because it was purely motivated. He wanted the best for them.

All of us have a hard time reaching that level of purity in our desires. Therefore, what we might want to call "righteous indignation" or "righteous anger" is mixed with selfish desires. But we can grow closer to that level of righteous indignation through our Godly Sorrow.

When we have true Godly Sorrow, we are motivated by the same love that motivated Jesus—a desire for someone else to enjoy the fruits of righteousness and avoid the destructive effects of sinful choices. Jesus didn't make it about himself, even though he was being rejected and, of all people, he should have received the respect he deserved. He never took ungodly behavior personally. Instead, he grieved for the pain it caused others.

Let's look at some other biblical examples of Godly Sorrow.

Ruth

Naomi, Ruth's mother-in-law, was a pitifully depressed person. Although Naomi was not sinning against Ruth, certainly Ruth would have preferred being around someone who was cheerful. But Ruth did not require anything from Naomi that Naomi could not give. She clung to her and identified with her— Naomi's God would be Ruth's God, even though Naomi was not representing her God very well. Ruth was gracious and loving. She must have been sad that Naomi was sad, but she did not respond in frustration or try to change her. In time, Ruth was honored and Naomi rose out of her depression. Ruth's thoughts of Surrender may have been, "Even if my needs aren't met, I'll trust this God whom Naomi represents."

The Apostle Paul

Paul wrote, "I am speaking the truth in Christ—I am not lying; my conscience bears me witness in the Holy Spirit— that I have great sorrow and unceasing anguish in my heart. For I could wish that I myself were accursed and cut off from Christ for the sake of my brothers, my kinsmen according to the flesh" (Rom. 9:1–3). Although Paul has been attacked, blamed, and physically hurt by some of the people he is grieving over, he would give up his own salvation if that could bring them to salvation. He does not take their rejection of Christ as a personal attack on himself.

King David

During that time when King David was escaping Jerusalem after Absalom had usurped his kingship, he was physically assaulted by Shimei, who threw rocks at him. David's defenders wanted to kill Shimei, but here we see David's heart of Surrender:

> David said to Abishai and to all his servants, "Behold, my own son seeks my life; how much more now may this Benjaminite! Leave him alone, and let him curse, for the LORD has told him to. It may be that the LORD will look on the wrong done to me, and that the LORD will repay me with good for his cursing today" (2 Sam. 16:11–12).

When we Surrender, we trust God enough to say, "Even if I'm hurt by this person when I am vulnerable before them, I will trust you, God, that you will not allow anything that is not for your glory and my good."

Even though we may have such a heart of Surrender, that still doesn't mean there should not be boundaries. It does not mean we must allow anything and everything to happen to us, as if another person should dictate what we deserve. We should seek God's direction, wisdom, and strength to find out and to fulfill his plan and purposes. God may not want us to expose ourselves to harm. If you are in an abusive relationship, you should take action to remove yourself and receive help from others. Knowing God's will for godly boundaries takes a lot of guidance. We must be aware if Wounds, Messages, Vows, and Strategies are contributing to our being a victim.

Gary Thomas writes,

> Earlier in my life, I worked with a bully. I began praying that God would help me see the insecurity behind his bravado. My temptation is always to look at what someone is doing to me. God-sight is about being less self-obsessed and learning to see the situation as God sees it, in its totality. Yes, God loves me and doesn't want me to be tyrannized—but he also loves the bully and wants him to repent.

Choosing Godly Sorrow is a challenge because when we are attacked, misunderstood, or hurt, everything within us wants to fight to stay in control of the situation or to defend ourselves. 2 Corinthians 7:1–9 gives us some insights into living in the Holy Spirit's power in this area.

> Since we have these promises, beloved, let us cleanse ourselves from every defilement of body and spirit, bringing holiness to completion in the fear of God.
>
> Make room in your hearts for us. We have wronged no one, we have corrupted no one, we have taken advantage of no one. I do not say this to condemn you, for I said before that you are in our hearts, to die together and to live together. I am acting with great boldness toward you; I have great pride in you; I am filled with comfort. In all our affliction, I am overflowing with joy. . . .
>
> For even if I made you grieve with my letter, I do not regret it—though I did regret it, for I see that that

letter grieved you, though only for a while. As it is, I rejoice, not because you were grieved, but because you were grieved into repenting. For you felt a godly grief, so that you suffered no loss through us.

Let's see these four points:

- Paul's goal is always cleansing that leads to holiness.
- Paul's motive is being at peace with everyone.
- Paul's desire is to reconcile and encourage, not to condemn.
- Paul affirms his love for them regardless of their faults.

Paul's pure motive of Godly Sorrow comes through clearly. He wants them to come to Repentance through their own Godly Sorrow about their sins. We all have the Spirit's power to enable us to make that godly choice and not get Hooked by those who hurt us.

Love Well

When we Surrender to trusting God, we will be able to love others *well*. We stress that word "well." All of us love others imperfectly. But loving "well" means we love them for their benefit rather than for what it does for us or how it makes us look. We are not talking here about perfection, but we are talking about desiring another's good. We have all been around someone who supposedly is expressing love for us, but it is disingenuous because it is really all about them looking good. We don't really feel encouraged or cared for.

I (Larry) may be wrong, but I sensed a lack of loving well when I received an email from a man who was considering buying one of our marriage books for his wife. He wrote, "I chose to love my unsaved wife as I love myself. She has a lot of issues, and it's my hope, prayer and confidence that my example, the light that I allow to shine in our home, and the love that I extend to her, just as God has done for me, will be a part of what God uses to save her."

I did not have any kind of relationship with this man to be able to inquire into his motives. But I could sense that he might easily come across to his wife as thinking himself better than her. I wondered if he communicated a belief that he never needed to repent of anything and that she should be grateful for the way he puts up with her.

And I also wondered, "What is his motive for needing to explain this to me?" Does he speak to others with this same kind of superior attitude? If his wife shared with him the superior attitudes she senses, how would he respond? I had a deep sense that he was not loving her *well*. Unfortunately, he had concluded that since he loved her so well, he was amazed that his sparkling and pristine example of Christ's love had not compelled her to become a Christian.

Here are some other common ways we do not love well and do not Surrender because it is really all about us.

A husband buys his wife for their anniversary (or birthday or Christmas) what he wants for himself, not what she values. He looks forward to the admiring looks from his friends when he uses the item himself.

A wife plans an elaborate surprise birthday party for her husband, when actually he would delight in a weekend away with her. But the accolades the wife gets at the party motivates her to throw another party the next year.

Let us examine our own hearts to make sure they are Surrendered to whatever God wants to do so that we can love others *well*.

See the Spiritual Battle

In order to have Godly Sorrow and love others well, we should recognize the spiritual battle that is being waged for their souls.

Remember the story of Peter rebuking Jesus in Matthew 16:21–23?

> From that time Jesus began to show his disciples that he must go to Jerusalem and suffer many things from the elders and chief priests and scribes, and be killed, and on the third day be raised. And Peter took him aside and began to rebuke him, saying, "Far be it from you, Lord! This shall never happen to you." But he turned and said to Peter, "Get behind me, Satan! You are a hindrance to me. For you are not setting your mind on the things of God, but on the things of man."

Jesus knew the spiritual battle going on for Peter's mind. Satan most likely hoped that Jesus would become discouraged. Jesus could have thought, *Peter just doesn't understand me or the Father's plan, even after all the time I've spent with him. I'd hoped my training would have made more of an impact. What will other people think of my teaching?*

We can't even imagine Jesus having such thoughts. Instead he saw the heavenly battle. Like Jesus, we will be able to love well if we see the spiritual battle going on instead of making it about us as we defend ourselves. Then we will be able to

Surrender, saying, "Even if I am misunderstood (or whatever is going on), I'll trust that God can bring truth into this situation that is being influenced by Satan."

Satan knows your Wounds, Messages, Vows, and Strategies. He is going to try to Hook you. To help us Surrender, we must believe that God is sovereign and allows only that which is for our good. Then we can care about the needs of someone else and what is best for them. That is having Godly Sorrow and loving them well.

And in some instances we may see the result of repentance like David saw in Saul after David resisted taking Saul's life in the cave (1 Sam. 24). In that story we see how David had Godly Sorrow about Saul's sin and loved him well. As a result, Saul declared, "You are more righteous than I, for you have repaid me good, whereas I have repaid you evil. And you have declared this day how you have dealt well with me, in that you did not kill me when the LORD put me into your hands" (24:17–18).

It may be that David's Surrender was fueled by, "Even if my becoming king is delayed, I will trust God's plan."

Ability to Forgive

Surrender brings a desire to forgive those who have wounded us. This is not an easy subject, nor something easy for any of us to choose. But inspired by the grace we receive from God, which includes receiving his forgiveness and cleansing, we can forgive others. As we have said earlier in this book, our own sin is just as bad as anyone else's. We stand on level ground at the cross. All of us stand condemned equally before God. Sin is sin. It doesn't take any more power from God to forgive what we would call a "big" sin. Yes, the consequences on earth of some sins are greater, but regardless, Jesus took every one of them to the cross.

Remember how we stressed David's thought in Psalm 51 that his sin was against God *only*? "Against you, you only, have I sinned and done what is evil in your sight," David prayed. The person who hurt you and whom you find so hard to forgive, sinned against God, just as you have hurt others and have also sinned against God. Knowing that God is a God of justice can give you the peace to know that he will not let any wound you have suffered go unpunished. His justice is far more significant and consequential than your anger, which only hurts yourself. Romans 12:19 assures us, "Beloved, never avenge yourselves, but leave it to the wrath of God, for it is written, 'Vengeance is mine, I will repay, says the Lord.'" God, your Father, calls you Beloved and wants to quiet your heart with the assurance that he will take care of you.

Additionally, remember:

- Forgiving does not mean the wound was not hurtful or important.
- Forgiving does not mean we should necessarily subject ourselves to further harm.
- Forgiving does not mean we release those who abuse or misuse us from consequences of their sin.

Obviously, whole books have been written about forgiveness, books that contain so many more important concepts, but let us close this subject by summarizing three points that Dan Allender makes in his book, *The Wounded Heart,* about how forgiveness and Surrender result in: hunger for restoration, bold love, and revoked revenge.

Hunger for Restoration

So many find it impossible to picture having a relationship with the offending person. But it is possible after surrendering to God and desiring the good of that person. Allender writes, "A heart that knows something of the joy of returning to God will be drawn to offer restoration like God." This is not an easy path, and it won't be accomplished quickly. Neither should it be attempted in every situation. Allender is right when he says, "The ability to imagine what the abuser could be if he repented and was redeemed opens the way to hunger for a pure and righteous restoration of relationship."

Bold Love

Allender explains, *"Love is a powerful force and energy to reclaim the potential good in another, even at the risk of great sacrifice and loss"* (italics in original). Like the Loving Well we examined earlier, bold love desires the best for the other person. And it is also motivated by facing our own sin, knowing that we all equally deserve God's wrath, regardless of the seriousness of our sin. When we remember the forgiveness, cleansing, and joy we received from God based upon his grace and not our performance, we can see another person—even the person hurting us—through God's eyes.

But please know that it is not contradictory to love someone, desire their good, and equally work toward destroying their sin cancer by bringing them to repentance and faith.

Revoked Revenge

When we have been hurt, our natural—not supernatural—response is to take revenge in some way, to react in the same hurtful way, to blame, accuse, be self-righteous . . . and the list

200

goes on to include so many possible sinful reactions that don't honor God. But what does honor God? The wisdom of Romans 12:19–21 urges us:

> Beloved, never avenge yourselves, but leave it to the wrath of God, for it is written, "Vengeance is mine, I will repay, says the Lord." To the contrary, "if your enemy is hungry, feed him; if he is thirsty, give him something to drink; for by so doing you will heap burning coals on his head." Do not be overcome by evil, but overcome evil with good.

"The desire to do harm to another is not always the same as wanting him to pay for his sin," Allender writes. "Many times I have prayed for harm to come to a blind, arrogant, harmful man or woman in order to bring them to their senses."

Knowing God's leading in such difficult circumstances requires much wisdom and guidance from others. But we can trust God's empowering to Surrender and act in godly ways.

Continue to Say "Even If . . ."

When I was a boy in Sunday School, I remember protecting myself from the ridicule of others about my poor public reading skills. It would just kill me when the teacher would have the group read a passage of Scripture by asking each student to read one verse, going around the circle. I was always grateful when the reading order allowed me to count ahead. I would find "my" verse and then recount to make sure I didn't miscount. Then, oblivious to the content of the material, I would read in my mind each word of my verse over and over. It helped me to feel in control.

Even now I can vividly remember the tension that quivered inside me as a seven-year-old boy. I can still feel the fear that grabbed my gut. I must not be exposed as weak—and this was before my acting fiasco! I can see now that my self-protection skills started early. But they still affect me today.

I attend a weekly men's Bible study. At the start of each lesson the teacher calls on one of us to open in prayer. I can remember thinking, "Call on me, please. I have something to share that is rich." Why was that? Because I always came prepared with some Scripture and a written prayer. I remember thinking this was good stuff that would edify us all.

My prepared prayer was even more important to me because, on occasion, I would fill in for that teacher. I wanted to protect my position and image. I needed to be thought of well by those men so that when I taught the lesson my words would be well regarded.

But as Kathy and I worked on this chapter and I connected the dots between that little boy who read ahead and practiced his assigned verse, I could see that I was protecting myself from feeling out of control and being seen as weak at that men's Bible study.

It is amazing how God works in our lives. I remember hearing Paul David Tripp say, "God will take you where you haven't chosen to go in order to produce in you what you could not achieve on your own." Even memories of our past, memories that still affect our behaviors and choices today, can be used to stimulate us to deeper levels of Repentance and Surrender.

It was clear to me that God wanted me to feel the weight of my sin against him when I used my position more for my glory than his. This was a painful moment. I wanted to magnify my image of a mature Christian leader in the eyes of those men.

Just like the little boy, I was determined to ensure that others thought well of me and my position.

When I became aware of my sin, I asked God to forgive me, and I surrendered by not going to class with a prepared prayer. I prayed, "Lord, even if I'm seen in a negative light and not regarded as a strong Christian, I will trust that you know what you're doing. I will cry out to you in prayer, in that moment trusting your leading. You know how to minister to the needs of others. I'll trust in that."

The way to counteract Wounds, Messages, Vows, and Strategies after we repent of our sin is to say, "Even if . . ." while trusting God to do whatever he wants.

Reflections and Group Discussion Questions

1. When you saw the chapter title "Surrender," what did you first think of?

2. Generally speaking, how easy or difficult is it for you to Surrender to God? Explain.

3. We define Surrender as saying "Even if . . ." How would you describe it?

4. How important is God's sovereignty to you in fostering greater Surrender?

5. Of the description of God written by Adam Clarke, which characteristic is most meaningful to you? Why?

6. How would you define Godly Sorrow in your own words?

7. Does the concept of Godly Sorrow help you in any way? How?

8. Who do you need to love *well*? Can you identify the reason(s) that you haven't been able to love that person well? What might it look like now?

9. Does thinking of the spiritual battle occurring in the life of the person whom you react to wrongly help in any way? What does Satan have to gain by gaining the allegiance of that person?

10. What has been a block in the past (or present) to forgiving another person? What do you find helpful from the three points in that section?

Chapter 10

The Process

Our union with Christ allows us to have two confidences that are the empowering mechanisms for godliness in the Christian life: 1) confidence that our status does not change; and, 2) confidence that our ability does change.

—Bryan Chapell

Pain in this world is a foregone conclusion. The only question is whether we choose to live a life of redemptive pain or of self-destructive pain.

—Gary Thomas

This past year I have been slowly recovering from a shoulder injury. After a period of nine months, the physical therapy relieved me of 90 percent of the problem and pain. The therapists gave me some exercises I could perform at home to assist in the recovery. I didn't care for the extra time they took, and I felt pretty good anyway, so I chose not to continue them on my own, especially since traveling and insurance glitches interrupted my office visits for about five weeks.

At the end of the five weeks, the intense pain returned, and I complained to Kathy. She responded, "Would you like a little cheese with that whine? Don't you remember that the therapist said your injury might require home exercises for the rest of your life?"

I muttered some acknowledgment of that statement but whined some more, "I used to bounce back so quickly from injuries like this. Why can't it be like that now?"

She lovingly looked at me and said, "Honey, you can never go back to your younger self. You have to continue supporting the health of your shoulder for the rest of your life if you want to keep the pain away."

All of us want to keep the pain away, whether it is emotional, physical, spiritual, or mental pain. And we believe that the principles you have learned in this book can help you to draw closer to God, who is the only true source of living in holiness. Which is the right way to view pain: as a means to holiness.

But there are no instant fixes for becoming holy. God, at times, provides an instantaneous deliverance from a sin pattern, but most of the time he wants us to continue to grow more dependent on him through a Process of Growth, which is what this last chapter is about.

Holiness Involves a Process

Is this a shocking thought to you, that holiness involves a Process? After all, it may seem like once we know our Wound, Message, Vow, and Strategy, we'll always be empowered to choose holiness—*perfectly*.

Unfortunately, this is not true, and for good reasons. If we could be perfect on this earth, we would not need God, and we would most likely be judgmental because other people are not perfect like us. Basically, our perfection would become another kind of Strategy to leave out God! Isn't that a crazy thought? You would think our perfection on this earth would bring glory to God, but it would most likely only give glory to ourselves.

Yet, we can become discouraged when we struggle with a Strategy over and over again. And even more importantly, we struggle with thinking that God wants us to become perfect, and therefore he's discouraged with us too. But let's look at some verses which will assure us that God wants to patiently work with us without the expectation that we will conquer every struggle immediately.

"I am sure of this," Paul said, "that he who began a good work in you will bring it to completion at the day of Jesus Christ" (Phil. 1:6). We think it should read "bring it to completion *yesterday*," but we will only be "completed" on the day when Jesus comes back or the day when we see Jesus in heaven.

"Practice these things, immerse yourself in them, so that all may see your progress" (1 Tim. 4:15). You would think it should read "so that all may see your *perfection*," but it doesn't. Progress keeps us depending on God for growth. We must "practice."

"By one sacrifice he has made perfect forever those who are being made holy" (Heb. 10:14 NIV). Notice the verbs? We are *made* perfect through Jesus' sacrifice forever (in our position in Christ) even while we are *being* made holy while living on this earth (that's the Process of Growth).

Knowing who we are in Christ (our position) is essential for us to be encouraged as we are sanctified (the process of becoming more holy). Being in Christ is not something we earn through our own goodness. It is a part of the package of the gospel of grace that we are given as a child of God. Since we could not earn it, we cannot lose it. And it should motivate us to want to grow and love God more . . . and more.

Who are you "in Christ"?

- Having grace: Ephesians 2:8
- Strong: Philippians 4:13
- Having the mind of Christ: 1 Corinthians 2:16
- Peaceful: John 14:27
- Justified: Romans 5:1
- Receiving mercy, therefore prayers are heard: Hebrews 4:16
- Chosen: Ephesians 1:3–4
- Blessed: Ephesians 1:3
- Redeemed: Ephesians 1:7
- Important: 1 Peter 1:18–19
- Forgiven: Ephesians 1:7
- Regenerated: Titus 3:5
- Adopted: Galatians 4:5–7
- Having a new name: Revelation 3:12
- Holy: Colossians 1:22
- Righteous: Ephesians 4:24
- Blameless: Ephesians 1:4
- Sealed with Holy Spirit: Ephesians 1:13–14
- New creature: 2 Corinthians 5:17

What an incredible list! And there is even more because of our union with Christ. Incredibly, we do not earn any of those inheritances. All these benefits are gifts from God bestowed on us because of our salvation. What a glorious way to remind ourselves that we are loved, valued, and empowered to be sanctified, drawing closer and closer to our precious Lord.

Although all of those benefits and blessings totally belong to every Christian, we must learn to "walk" in the truth of each one. And that is the Process of sanctification.

Knowing who we are in Christ can motivate us to respond in obedience, not because we are obligated, but out of gratitude for the incredible mercy we have received. We don't deserve any of the blessings that our inheritance in Christ affords us. It is all because of God's gracious gifts to us.

This was abundantly made clear to me (Kathy) some time ago when I deserved a traffic ticket. I was driving down a California freeway on a superbly beautiful day of fluffy clouds on a background of clear blue sky, and I just felt extra happy. My happiness pressed my foot against the accelerator as the wind from the open window blew through my hair. I didn't see the highway patrolman until the red lights from his cruiser grabbed my attention and I pulled over to the side of the road.

He came up to my side of the car, and we went through the regular questions. Then I said, "I don't expect you to not write a ticket, but my husband will ask me if I told you that he's an officer in Huntington Beach." I gave him Larry's name.

He didn't smile as he took my license and walked back to his car. I knew I was getting a ticket, and I knew I deserved it. I had nothing to complain about.

As I waited, it seemed like he was taking a long time but, thankfully, I had never received a moving violation before, so I did not really know how long it took.

Then he emerged from his car and walked up to mine. He handed me my license and said, "Next time drive the speed limit."

I melted in gratitude and said, "Thank you." I didn't know if he had checked to see if Larry was an officer, but I didn't care. I did not have to pay a fine and a bad mark wasn't added to my record.

After I drove off, I slowly worked my way back into traffic and was surprised at my reaction. I drove below the speed limit.

And I wanted to try to find the officer again on the road and shout, "See? I'm so grateful that I now want to obey the law. Thank you so much for your mercy!"

I have never forgotten that experience, primarily because it shouts to me of how growing more sanctified and thus obedient should come from gratitude for the mercy and grace God gives us. Just as I "knew" someone who could qualify me to avoid that ticket, our identity with Christ qualifies us to avoid the wrath and punishment we deserve for our sin. And then out of the strong gratitude for the fact that we have not received what we deserve, we say, "Look, Lord! I'm so grateful that I want to show it by obeying you."

Warning!

As much as we believe that seeking out the Wounds, Messages, Vows, and Strategies is significant for bringing a heart change, we fear lest someone become obsessed with discovering the underlying reasons for their sin. If that happens, they could halt sanctification because they believe they must find the underlying reasons before they can make changes in their behavior. We could be excessively introspective rather than focusing on the gospel and making a decision to obey regardless of whether we know the underlying causes of our Strategy.

That is not our desire as we share these ideas. Many times we simply cannot identify the Wound, Message, Belief, and Vow. The Spirit of God has not revealed them. We might be tempted to think that then we can't change. But the Spirit of God is not held captive by models or plans, not even by ours. He can work by drawing us to his living spring with or without man-made ideas.

So please don't be obsessed with trying to figure it out. Yes, do evaluate. Yes, do ask God to reveal what he wants to reveal. But don't think that you can't draw closer to God until you have discovered the underlying reasons. Sometimes we just need to say, "Have mercy, Lord. I don't know why I keep doing this."

It is then that we can ask God's forgiveness and claim his promise in Psalm 138:8: "The LORD will fulfill his purpose for me; your steadfast love, O LORD, endures forever. Do not forsake the work of your hands."

Our friend told us, "I've often thought while going through something difficult, if I could only learn what God wants me to learn, then the trial would get over faster. So I try to analyze and figure it out, but it sure doesn't work that way. Sometimes we just have to experience something and trust him. In his time he reveals himself to us. It always makes more sense to us later."

We also need to avoid thinking, "If I just learn what God wants me to learn, I'll get the desires of my heart." Maybe that "desire" is to be married or for our prodigal to be saved. It could be our health being restored or being hired for our dream job. Whatever it is, we become motivated to obey in order to have an easier life. But in cases like this we are only trying to manipulate God instead of trusting him for the journey.

These are temptations for all of us, but we can resist them by trusting God's sovereign timing and loving care for us. Relax in whatever way he chooses to work and to reveal whatever he desires. He can be trusted.

Whirlpool of Growth

Once we know the foundation of our spiritual heritage as sons and daughters of the King, we can apply principles that will encourage this growth Process of walking in our position in

Christ. So let's look at some specific tools we can use to put our knowledge of Wounds, Message, Vows, and Strategies into practice and possibly to prevent us from being Hooked and needing to Repent.

An important concept is how we envision this growth Process of sanctification. Most of us think of it visually like a linear timeline. On the left side of the line we make a step of progress and the temptation is now in the past—we think—and we will never need to address it again. We believe we have moved along that line to the right, so we will only encounter new challenges, not old ones.

But that is not an accurate visual map of change. Change is more like a spiral. Let's call it a whirlpool. Doesn't life seem like that at times? We are going around and around and every time we reach a certain area, a rock, representing one of our Strategies, hits us. In our spiritual walk, the rock represents a temptation to be Hooked. If we think there are no rocks (as if they are behind us in a timeline), we will be surprised and unaware of their approach.

But knowing that we have the tendencies of a particular Strategy, we can see that rock in the whirlpool coming at us. Instead of being knocked around by it, we can actually chip off a piece by laying hold of God's power and resisting the temptation. Little by little, as chip by chip comes off that rock, it becomes smaller and smaller until it disappears—or at least grows so little that the temptation is easily resisted.

Unfortunately, the whirlpool of life reveals new rocks in different places. And so, as we identify the reasons for the rock (our Wounds, Messages, Idols, and Strategies), we will go through the Process of gradually chipping off its hold on us. As the Process continues, we can more easily see the rock approaching.

But we will also become more aware of deeper levels of sin. We may think growth should eliminate our awareness of sin, but it only makes it more glaring. Pastor John MacArthur, Jr., says, "Let me warn you that the more victory you experience as you mature in Christ, the more you will recognize sin in your life."

Romans 13:14 gives us the challenge to "put on the Lord Jesus Christ, and make no provision for the flesh, to gratify its desires." When we make no provision for the flesh—for that rock of temptation, we figure out why it is attractive to us (our Idol), and we recognize what we are trying to do to prevent pain. Then we can Repent and Surrender, which will possibly empower us to avoid the rock altogether or to continue chipping off pieces until it is not there at all.

In addition, 1 Corinthians 10:13 promises us, "No temptation has overtaken you that is not common to man. God is faithful, and he will not let you be tempted beyond your ability, but with the temptation he will also provide the way of escape, that you may be able to endure it."

At times when we succumb to being thrown around by a rock in the whirlpool, we wonder, "Didn't God promise there would be a way of escape?" It is confusing to us because we don't feel like we had any help. But, by being honest as we look back, we can recognize God's help was there, but we either did not want the help or we set ourselves up for failure. Consider Michael Olan Webb's thoughts.

> Near the city where I live, there's a range of moun-
> tains with a series of beautiful canyons, stretching
> like fingers into the high Arizona desert. Carr Canyon
> is one of these, where, during the spring thaw and
> rainy seasons, there's an 800-foot waterfall that can

be seen for miles around. Carr Falls is a popular hikers' destination and is frequently a hangout for young people. At the top of the falls, there are barriers and signs warning that proceeding past that threshold, even when the rocks appear dry, can be deadly. There is lichen growing on those dry rocks—laden with invisible moisture—which, crushed underfoot, releases lubrication that can make a slide unstoppable.

Many years ago, a young adventurer decided to go past the threshold. The water wasn't running . . . the rocks appeared dry; and so, spurred on by the hubris of youth, he stepped over the barrier while his friends watched. He was sure he could stop any possible slide; he could gamble and beat the odds. But the odds were against him and, tragically, he lost. And his family and friends lost him.

Our own delusional hubris may try to convince us that we can beat the odds.

Slow Down the Reaction

Another important coping tip is to slow down! It sounds so simple and "small," but it is essential. So much of the time when we are Hooked into sin, it is because we react without seeking God. We just react, believing that we have no other choice, or believing that our perception of what is occurring is correct. But knowing about the elements we have been studying can help us to reconsider our "natural" reaction and ask God to give us clarity to discern his "supernatural" reaction.

Consider Zechariah 4:10: "For whoever has despised the day of small things shall rejoice, and shall see the plumb line in the hand of Zerubbabel."

At the time of Zechariah's writing, some older people were unimpressed with the construction of the new Temple. They remembered the old Temple that had been destroyed early in their lifetime. They had seen that magnificent Temple built by Solomon; to them this replacement did not compare. They called the new construction "a small thing," but God (through Zechariah) says, "Who is calling my work 'small'? Anything I do is big!" That is also his message through the prophet Haggai:

> Who is left among you who saw this house in its
> former glory? How do you see it now? Is it not
> as nothing in your eyes? Yet now be strong, O
> Zerubbabel, declares the LORD. Be strong, O Joshua,
> son of Jehozadak, the high priest. Be strong, all you
> people of the land, declares the LORD. Work, for I am
> with you, declares the LORD of hosts. . . . The latter
> glory of this house shall be greater than the former,
> says the LORD of hosts. And in this place I will give
> peace, declares the LORD of hosts (2:3–4, 9).

Here are some "small" thoughts.

- Small doesn't mean meaningless.
- What seems small is often the beginning of something big for God.
- God values "small" because then he is glorified when it brings great results.
- God chooses weak vessels so that he will be glorified.
- Your first step is important. Don't give up.
- Small steps add up.

Earlier I shared with you how I struggled while taking care of Larry's mom, Audrey. In the two and a half years she lived with us before her death, God did a mighty work in me (actually in both of us) to help us learn and grow in so many ways. I learned to slow down my reactions and work through what was really going on inside me. Little by little I grew in my ability to listen to the Holy Spirit asking me questions about my motives. Quite often those questions helped me see how I was leaving God out of my life and trying to live on my own terms.

I remember one morning when Audrey was eating her bran cereal. Every morning I had to soak the cereal in milk for at least thirty minutes to make it soft. But on this particular morning the delusion of her Lewy body dementia was "alive."

She said to me, "There are rocks in my cereal. I know you're trying to kill me."

I could feel the hair on the back of my neck begin to rise. But I stopped myself, and prayed quickly, "Lord, this is my old pattern of wanting to be approved and not wanting to be seen as undependable. I'm going to pause because I know in Christ I am dependable, loved, and approved."

I did relax, but I was not ready for what happened next.

Audrey mumbled something else and then said, "And I wish you'd do a better job of it."

Of course, she meant that I should make her cereal better—meaning without rocks. But the juxtaposition of her remarks was funny. I should do a better job of killing her? I stifled a laugh and wasn't upset—for once!

Another morning she shuffled down the hall toward me, exclaiming, "Don't lie to me. You attacked me last night!"

Oh! That is one of my hot buttons—to be called a liar. I so wanted to be mean in return, but again I slowed down my reaction and prayed, asking God to help me see myself as he sees me—as a daughter of the King. The Lord gave me compassion for Audrey, who was also a daughter of the King, even when she was mentally driven by dementia. Her words did not bother me in the least. God was doing a work in me of "small things," and although I still reacted in unloving ways at times, those reactions diminished as the months slipped by. The rock in the whirlpool was being chipped off.

Now I am the primary caregiver for my own mother, even though she does not live in our home. The truth God revealed about my Wounds, Messages, Vows, and Strategies during the time I cared for my mother-in-law now empowers me to love my own mother better. At times, I am tempted in the "old ways," because there are still rocks in the whirlpool, but I am not getting Hooked as much as I was with Audrey.

James 4:1–3 gives us a warning about those rocks. "What causes quarrels and what causes fights among you? Is it not this, that your passions are at war within you? You desire and do not have, so you murder. You covet and cannot obtain, so you fight and quarrel. You do not have, because you do not ask. You ask and do not receive, because you ask wrongly, to spend it on your passions." These verses refer to our underlying motives for sinful reactions: wanting, coveting, and wrong asking because we demand that our desires be fulfilled. What we think we need for happiness, security, and love is being withheld from us, and we believe we must fight to have them.

In his book *Marriage Matters: Extraordinary Change through Ordinary Moments*, Winston T. Smith applies those verses to marriage, "Frustrated or blocked desires battle within you. When I'm fighting with my wife, usually I want something that I'm not getting. . . . As you try to figure out how you're contributing to the quarrel, the Bible suggests that you ask yourself a question: 'What do I want?'"

That's an important idea for any area of life. And asking questions like this helps us to slow down our reaction. Here are some further questions along that line:

- What do I want?
- What do I fear?
- What am I trying to avoid?
- How is this ignoring God?
- How do I think this will get what I want?

These questions can help you to slow down and resist being Hooked.

How to Slow Down

How can we slow down? As I (Kathy) teach parenting classes, the subject of a child's bed-wetting sometimes comes up, and I'm able to tell them about the "Wee Alert." The first parent who told me about this product bought it because her daughter could not overcome bed-wetting. She seemed excited that it worked.

This mother told us that the Wee Alert is comprised of a thin metal plate that is put on the child's bed underneath the bottom sheet. Then a corner of it is hooked up to a little machine. When moisture hits the plate, it sends a current to the machine, which then sounds an alarm. Of course, no electrical current touches the child. For the first few nights when the alarm went off, this mama said, the little girl continued to sleep. Of course, they had to go through the process of changing sheets, but then the girl went back to sleep. Her parents wondered how it was ever going to make a difference.

But eventually, one night after the alarm sounded for a little while, the girl woke up. And the next night, she woke up a little sooner. Several nights later, she woke up right after the alarm began sounding. And two nights later, she woke up as she was wetting herself. The next night she woke up in time to go to the bathroom. After that she had some accidents, but they became fewer and fewer. And finally, she never wet the bed again.

The Wee Alert had worked.

As crude an example as that is, it demonstrates what growth can look like. Something happens and we get Hooked. We got Hooked because we may have feared being seen a certain way or our Idol was threatened. Whatever we feared losing in that moment prompted us to react with our Self-Protective Strategy. We reacted without taking it to the Lord, and we didn't allow the Holy Spirit to empower us or reveal our Strategy. But after a while, if we asked the Lord to reveal what was really going on inside us (like "Sitting in It"), the Spirit revealed our Strategy. Symbolically, we will need to "change the sheets" by Repenting, Surrendering, and apologizing if appropriate.

Then a similar incident occurs, the rock in the whirlpool of life throws us off course, and we are Hooked. But this time we calm down sooner, and take it to the Lord sooner, and we Repent and Surrender more quickly. (And apologize with more conviction.)

As we develop our coping skills, when we are tempted to be Hooked, we learn to see the rock coming and seek the Lord to reveal the Idol and Strategy. And we also remind ourselves of our position in Christ. As a result, we respond in a supernatural way in the Spirit's power. We choose wisely, and his fruit is the outcome.

But we are not perfect. The next time we are tempted, we might fail. We must "change the sheets" by repenting, confessing, being cleansed and forgiven. But that is all right, because God's grace is sufficient, and another failure does not mean we are hopeless. It only means that God is continuing to peel away deeper layers of Strategies.

In fact, as you gain insight into what makes you tick, you may begin to be aware of more subtle ways you are sinning that you had not recognized before. As this has happened for us and for those we share these principles with, we start to become discouraged. It seems as if we are not making any headway at all.

This shows us, though, that we are becoming more sensitive to the Spirit's convicting power. It actually reveals that we are becoming more holy, because the more holy we are, the more we are aware of our sinful responses. God is working, and things that bothered us in the past may not bother us as much, but at the same time additional sinful patterns or responses are brought to our awareness. This is called sanctification.

Your Challenge

In Chapter Two, we talked about how we know when we are Hooked. We stated the opposite of each fruit of the Spirit described in Galatians 5:23–24. In the left column of this chart, you will find the wording we gave in that chapter. In the right blank column, we challenge you to apply a view in the Repentance, Surrender, and Process that you might be going through or want to go through.

The first chart gives an example.

Being Hooked	Repentance, Surrender, and Growth
Instead of being loving, we are apathetic, maybe even hateful. We rescue, people-please, and basically don't want the best for the other person. We withdraw or even punish through withdrawal.	Lord, I repent of my lack of desiring the good of others, and I surrender that even if my needs are not met, I will trust that you know what is best to meet my true needs. Help me to grow in my ability to put others above myself according to your plan.

Being Hooked	Repentance, Surrender, and Growth
Instead of being loving, we are apathetic, maybe even hateful. We rescue, people-please, and basically don't want the best for the other person. We withdraw or even punish through withdrawal.	
Instead of being joyful, we are unhappy, disgruntled, and ungrateful.	
Instead of being peaceful, we are unsettled, worried, and tense.	
Instead of being patient, we are frustrated and have unrealistic expectations.	
Instead of being kind, we are mean-spirited and critical, unsympathetic and lacking in compassion. Our actions are rough and disrespectful of a person's dignity.	
Instead of being good, we are selfish and self-centered, wanting our own way.	

Instead of being gentle, we are harsh and disregard the emotions and needs of others.	
Instead of being faithful, we are dishonest, disloyal, and undependable.	
Instead of having self control, we are reckless, out of control, and held in bondage by anything that seems to make our life better.	

We hope that thinking ahead like this might strengthen you to see the rocks in the whirlpool.

Skipping Our Way into Holiness

As we have traveled this road of holiness, we trust you have learned a different perspective. That new viewpoint is beautifully expressed by Charles Spurgeon:

> We call those things mercies which please us, ease us, suit our wants, and fall in with our cravings. Truly they are so, but not less gracious are those benefits which cross us, pain us, and lay us low. The tender love which chastises us, the gentle kindness which bruises us, the fond affection which crushes us to the ground—these we do not so readily recount; yet is there as much of divine love in a smart as in a sweet, as great a depth of tenderness in buffeting as in consoling. We must count our crosses, diseases and pains if we would number up our blessings. Doubtless it is a mercy to be spared affliction, but he would be a wise

man who should tell which of the two was the greater boon—to be for the present without chastisement or to be chastened. We judge that in either case it is well with the righteous, but we will not have a word said to the disparagement of affliction. Granted that the cross is very bitter, we maintain with equal confidence that it is also very sweet.

The more we accept those truths as God's way to transform us, the more joy we will find in our lives, and even in our sorrows. For they are the way to trusting God more and walking in holiness.

Have you ever wondered what holiness feels like? Malachi 4:2 expresses what God might like us to experience when we see the fruits of holiness that he is producing in our lives: "But for you who fear my name, the sun of righteousness shall rise with healing in its wings. You shall go out leaping like calves from the stall." The phrase "sun of righteousness shall rise" refers to the coming of Jesus, who will make it possible for us to be set free so that we can skip in joy.

Have you ever "skipped" in your spirit after recognizing that your trust in God had expanded to include forgiving someone who hurt you *because you recognize how much you have been forgiven*? Or when you have given grace by listening with understanding to a friend share a problem—even though she usually ignores you—*because you have experienced God's grace*? Or when you are able to rest calmly in a situation that normally drives you over the edge *because you know God is in charge*? Or when you manage to be patient when your child spills milk at the dinner table for the third time *because you know God has repeatedly been patient with you*?

Just imagine the sight of that calf skipping in freedom because it is no longer boxed in by the stall. The Amplified Bible expresses that skipping phrase, "And you shall go forth and gambol like calves [released] from the stall and leap for joy." Just think, we can leap for joy when we obey God and operate in his power. We are no longer fenced in and held in bondage by sinful patterns like worry, fear, selfishness, hate, resentment, and so many other binding things.

The NIV words it: "And you will go out and frolic like well-fed calves." Oh, to frolic like well-fed calves! Can't you just picture it? This calf isn't emaciated; instead it is healthy and well-nourished. It has drunk often from the fresh, flowing spring. It seems to be assured that all its real needs are supplied, and it is free from concern about receiving love and care.

For you and for us, this is the foundation of holiness: believing and trusting in God's sovereign love that provides everything we truly need; therefore, we do not need to demand it from people who are needy themselves.

But where does all this start? The background to Malachi gives us the answer. The Israelites were in another phase of disobedience, and Malachi gave God's prophecy to try to turn them back to God. After three chapters of rebuke, the final chapter predicts what will happen when they do turn back. Meditate on that promise again. "But for you who fear my name, the sun of righteousness shall rise with healing in its wings. You shall go out leaping like calves from the stall."

When God brings healing to his people, there is a feeling of joy about being set free. Healing brings holiness, and holiness brings joy. God heals us of our Wounds that have created wrong ideas about life, God, and people. We begin to view our circumstances and the people around us as opportunities to serve God by being a servant. Less and less our attitude is, "I want to be a servant only if my needs are also fulfilled." More and more our attitude is, "I'll be a servant for God's glory regardless of how my own needs are met."

We are still growing in this, of course, for as long as we live, but the joy that comes when we cooperate with God is like skipping out of a pen where we had been restrained. We do not obey in order to have that feeling, but how generous it is of God to give us the reward to bless us.

Are you like a calf encircled in some stall? Could your stall be bitterness, a critical spirit, a sense of entitlement, People-Pleasing, or self-absorption? Do you want to break free? In God's power you can, through Repentance and Surrender. Receive the healing. Get ready to leap, gambol, and frolic. God is opening the gate.

Reflections and Group Discussion Questions

1. What has been your attitude or beliefs about whether holiness involves a Process? What is your belief now after reading this chapter?

2. Of these three passages, which is most significant to you: Philippians 1:6, 1 Timothy 4:15, or Hebrews 10:14? Explain why.

3. Is thinking of your "position in Christ" important to you? Which item in the list of your inheritance is most meaningful for you? What wrong belief does this counteract?

4. If you thought of growth as a timeline, what was your thinking about sanctification (growth)?

5. When you think of growth as circling in a whirlpool, does it make any difference? Explain.

6. Reread Romans 13:14. What can you identify in your reactions as "making provision for the flesh"? How could you stop making "provision for the flesh" in that area?

7. What can you see now as getting too close to the edge of temptation? What do you plan to do to prevent that?

8. Which question in the "Slow Down the Reaction" section do you think would be most meaningful for you?

9. We began this book drawing our attention to the fruit of the Spirit, and we are ending it that way. Which area do you think you have grown in as a result of reading this book? Which fruit do you think you need to concentrate on in the coming weeks and months?

10. Describe how "skipping like a calf" would look for you?

Bibliography

Allender, Dan. *The Wounded Heart*. Colorado Springs: NavPress, 1990.

Bridges, Jerry. *Respectable Sins: Confronting the Sins We Tolerate*. Colorado Springs: NavPress, 2007.

Calvin, John. *Institutes of the Christian Religion*. 3.3.2. Orlando: Signalman Publishing, 2008.

Carter, Anthony. *Blood Work*. Orlando: Reformation Trust Publishing, 2013.

Chapell, Bryan. *Holiness by Grace: Delighting in the Joy That Is Our Strength*. Wheaton: Crossway Books, 2003.

Crabb, Larry. *Finding God*. Grand Rapids: Zondervan, 1993.

Fitzpatrick, Elyse. *Idols of the Heart: Learning to Long for God Alone*. Phillipsburg: P&R, 2001.

Goetz, Dave L. "Welcoming Limits," *Christianity Today*, December 2010: 53.

Goyer, Tricia. *Blue Like Play Dough*. Sisters: Multnomah, 2009.

Holcomb, Lindsey, and Justin Holcomb. *Rid of My Disgrace: Hope and Healing for Victims of Sexual Assault*. Wheaton: Crossway Books, 2011.

Horning, Cathy. "Cathy's Heart" blog. http://www.cathyhorning. com/cathys-heart/blog/rediscovering-joy/it-s-okay-to-cry/. Accessed May 29, 2013.

Kellemen, Robert W. *Spiritual Friends*. Winona Lake: BMH Books, 2005.

Keller, Tim. *The Freedom of Self-Forgetfulness: The Path to True Christian Joy*. Chorley, England: 10Publishing, 2012.

-. *Counterfeit Gods: The Empty Promises of Money, Sex, and Power, and the Only Hope That Matters*. New York: Dutton, 2009.

Kopp, Heather. "Sober Boots" blog. http://soberboots.com/ 2013/02/13/that-feels-like-love-2/. Accessed February 13, 2013.

Lewis, C. S. http://www.goodreads.com/quotes/615-we-are-not-necessarily-doubting-that-god-will-do-the. Accessed January 15, 2014.

MacArthur, John, quote. http://www.gty.org/resources/positions/ P13/freedom-from-sin. Accessed March 2, 2014.

Patrick, Amie. "Image, and the Gospel." http://thegospelcoalition. org/blogs/tgc/2013/09/23/eating-body-image-and-the-gospel/. Accessed September 23, 2013.

Piper, John. http://thinkonthisquotes.blogspot.com/2008/11/great-est-ethical-challenge.html. Accessed February 11, 2014.

Priolo, Lou. *Pleasing People: How Not to Be an Approval Junkie.* Phillipsburg: P&R, 2007.

Smith, Winston T. *Marriage Matters: Extraordinary Change through Ordinary Moments.* Greensboro: New Growth Press, 2010.

Sproul, R. C. *The Holiness of God.* Carol Stream: Tyndale, 1985.

Spurgeon, Charles. Quote found at http://www.reformation21. org/blog/2014/02/we-call-those-things-mercies.php. Accessed March 3, 2014.

Swindoll, Charles. *Stones of Remembrance, Bible Study Guide.* Anaheim: Insight for Living, 1988.

Tchividjian, Tullian. *Glorious Ruin: How Suffering Sets You Free.* Colorado Springs: David C. Cook, 2012

TerKeurst, Lysa. *Unglued, Making Wise Choices in the Midst of Raw Emotions.* Grand Rapids: Zondervan, 2012.

Thomas, Gary. *The Beautiful Fight: Surrendering to the Transforming Presence of God Every Day of Your Life.* Grand Rapids: Zondervan, 2007.

Thorn, Joe. *Note to Self: The Discipline of Preaching to Yourself.* Wheaton: Crossway Books, 2011.

Tripp, Paul David. *Forever: You Can't Live Without It.* Wheaton: Zondervan, 2011. Kindle edition.

-. *Instruments in the Redeemer's Hands: People in Need of Change Helping People in Need of Change.* Phillipsburg: P&R, 2002.

–. "Don't Confuse Knowledge and Success with Maturity." http://thegospelcoalition.org/blogs/tgc/2012/05/20/dont-confuse-knowledge-and-success-with-maturity/. Accessed May 20, 2012.

–. http://marshill.com/2013/08/12/the-difference-between-amazement-and-faith-paul-tripp-sermon-recap.

Vine, W. E. *Vine's Expository Dictionary of Old and New Testament Words*. Old Tappan: Revell, 1981.

Watson, Thomas. Scott McArthur@pastorSDG. Accessed October 18, 2013.

Webb, Michael Olan. http://bentmanwalking.me/2012/05/26/when-wormtongue-speaks-2-a-devotional/. Accessed May 26, 2012.

Wilkerson, Mike. *Redemption: Freed by Jesus from the Idols We Worship*. Wheaton: Crossway Books, 2011.

Woodley, Matthew. "Brokenness: The Door to God's Power," *Discipleship Journal*, September/October 2008.

Authors

Larry Miller and Kathy Collard Miller are popular speakers who have spoken individually and as a couple at conferences and retreats across the United States and in several countries abroad.

Kathy's numerous books include *Partly Cloudy with Scattered Worries, Women of the Bible—The Smart Guide to the Bible,* and *Why Do I Put So Much Pressure on Myself and Others?* Her articles have appeared in such magazines as *Decision, Today's Christian Woman,* and *Focus on the Family—MidLife.* Larry's books include *God's Vitamin "C" for the Spirit of Men* and *Men of the Bible—The Smart Guide to the Bible.* Larry and Kathy have coauthored several volumes.

Besides their writing and speaking ministry, the Millers are active lay counselors. Kathy serves on the teaching staff of CLASS (Christian Leaders, Authors, and Speakers Seminar). Larry retired as a police lieutenant in Huntington Beach, California. He frequently leads Bible studies and small groups for men.

The Millers have been married since 1970. They live in southern California. They have two grown children and one grandson.

Visit the Millers at www.LarryandKathy.com or at www.KathyCollardMiller.blogspot.com.

Praise for

Never Ever Be the Same

"Slowly. Prayerfully. Thoughtfully. That is the way readers must approach *Never Ever Be the Same*. Be prepared to be challenged. Be prepared to be changed. Be prepared to understand yourself like never before. Indeed, you will never ever be the same."

—Steph Beth Nickel, coauthor of *Living Beyond My Circumstances*

"Healing from the dark pit of brokenness and pain rests in the hope of the process. Larry and Kathy Miller capture the essence of the life long journey by exposing the core of brokenness, by embracing the difficult work that must be done, and by affirming the hope of experiencing authentic joy in this life. Wherever one may be in the journey, *Never Ever Be the Same* offers everyone the opportunity to return to the promise of their Belovedness, and to hold on tight. A must read for every follower of the King."

—Bill Harbeck, founder/director of Holding onto Hope Ministries, and author of *Shattered, One Man's Journey from Sexual Abuse* and *Love Goes Both Ways: Surrendering to the Truth of Dependence*

"In our 20 years' experience ministering to individuals and couples, never have we found a resource so thorough and practical in helping people face the wounds of their past, surrender them to God, and move into a healthier future, spiritually and emotionally. Let Larry and Kathy Miller guide you through this examination of self, the cross, and the grace and healing power of Christ, and you will never ever be the same."

—Hugh and Cindi McMenamin, 20-year veterans of pastoral ministry and co-authors of *When Couples Walk Together: 31 Days to a Closer Connection*

"Finally, a book that interprets my neurotic tendencies from a biblical perspective and calls me to new freedom in Christ! *Never Ever Be the Same* will help you get your head straight and put you back on the path to spiritual maturity."

—**David E. Fessenden,** publishing consultant and literary agent, author of *The Case of the Exploding Speakeasy*

"If you are looking for shallow encouragement or superficial self-help, don't buy this book. However, if you desire greater authenticity, deeper life change, and a more intimate relationship with Christ and those closest to you, *Never Ever Be the Same* is for you. The refreshingly vulnerable story of Larry and Kathy's journey into a life of inner freedom from self-protective strategies will woo and instruct you toward deeper transformation into the person God created you to be."

—**Fred Wevodau,** DMin, author of *The Navigators*

"Are you feeling 'stuck' in your personal or spiritual life? Have your past experiences or choices put a cloud over the joy you long for today? In *Never Ever Be the Same,* authors Larry Miller and Kathy Collard Miller honestly share their own past struggles and have given readers a transformational tool for changing their lives for the better. Don't miss this remarkable book! I highly recommend it for personal or for small group study."

—**Carol Kent,** speaker and author of *Unquenchable: Grow a Wildfire Faith that Will Endure Anything* (Zondervan)

"Are you frustrated, angry, depressed, exhausted, or just feeling trapped in a negative life cycle or frustrating relationship pattern? If you have ever wondered, 'Why did I do that?' or 'How can I get unstuck?' there is hope and help! The Millers offer a realistic, in-depth, step-by-step way out of the muck and mire of the daily grind. *Never Ever Be the Same* offers a plan for real change, lasting change, and change that will make you love your life! Open the pages of this book and begin the journey of transformation!"

—**Pam and Bill Farrel,** authors of 40 books, including *Men Are Like Waffles, Women Are Like Spaghetti* and the 10 Best Decisions series

"Kathy and Larry Miller do an outstanding job of blending their individual voices into a common thread of coaching and counseling the reader through a life changing process—he or she will never be the same. Both authors are open and vulnerable about their own rough spots in life. They discuss how discovering the root causes and motivations of why you do what you do can lead to a new you free of anger, anxiety, and apprehension. The Millers carefully back up all of their suggestions with Scripture and research. If you're ready for a life change, this book is for you!"

—**Janet Thompson,** speaker and author of 17 books, including the *Woman to Woman Mentoring* resources, *Face-to-Face Bible* study series, *Dear God, They Say It's Cancer,* and *Dear God, Why Can't I Have a Baby?* www.womantowomanmentoring.com

"If you're one who likes to be in control, if things people say about you hurt you years later, if you'd like to know why you do what you do and how you can change, then *Never Ever Be the Same* is for you. This book shows how you can take your wounds of the past and use them to gain a greater spiritual maturity and a closer walk with the Lord. As the authors state, 'Because we have God's power to live supernaturally, we *can* have a different perspective. Just think of the joy and freedom that would result!'"

—**Donna Clark Goodrich,** freelance proofreader and editor, and author of *The Freedom of Letting Go*

"Seldom do I have several aha! moments in one single book. But *Never Ever Be the Same* grabbed me. The profound insights blended with God's Word touched my soul. And as the content of each page sang truth into my past, issues I had missed for years were revealed. I recommend this book to seasoned Christians—those who seek answers and those who face unresolved issues. The rich biblical references and the transparency of the authors add a refreshing blend that captivates the reader."

—**Janet Perez Eckles,** international speaker and author of *Simply Salsa: Dancing Without Fear at God's Fiesta*

"Larry and Kathy Miller's vulnerability and wisdom invite readers to enter into the deeper places of their own stories to experience freedom and redemption in Jesus Christ. This book offers wonderful insight and application to how our past experiences impact our present reality and how Jesus offers us something better."
    —**Tracy Hanson,** LPGA Tour Professional, www.OutOfTheRough.org

"This book has been very eye-opening to vows and their effects on my life. I found myself on the pages of this book. I found the reasons for the anger that wells up within me. I will never ever be the same. A new me began the day I began to read this book. Thank you Kathy and Larry for being so transparent with your lives. It helped me to see the issues in my own."
    —**Arleen Clark**